THE MYSTERIES OF YESOD

OF YESOD

Foundations of the Spiritual Life

Translated from the French
Original title: LES MYSTÈRES DE IÉSOD
les fondements de la vie spirituelle

Original edition
© 1973, Éditions Prosveta Société coop. (Suisse)

© 1978, Éditions Prosveta S.A., ISBN 2-85566-100-5

© 1982, Éditions Prosveta S.A., ISBN 2-85566-109-9

Prosveta S.A – B.P.12 – 83601 Fréjus CEDEX (France)
ISBN 978-2-85566-109-4

Omraam Mikhaël Aïvanhov

THE MYSTERIES OF YESOD
Foundations of the Spiritual Life

Complete Works – Volume 7 AN

PROSVETA

Readers will better understand certain aspects of the lectures published in the present volume if they bear in mind that Master Omraam Mikhaël Aïvanhov's teaching was exclusively oral and that the editors have made every effort to respect the flavour and style of each lecture.

The Master's teaching is more than a body of doctrines; it is an organic whole, and his way of presenting it was to approach it from countless different points of view. By treating certain aspects in many different contexts he constantly reveals a new dimension of the whole, and at the same time throws new light on the individual aspects and their vital links with each other.

Omraam Mikhaël Aïvanhov

TABLE OF CONTENTS

Part I

YESOD REFLECTS THE VIRTUES
OF ALL THE SEPHIROTH

Human beings fill their lives with all kinds of things, work and study, travel, sport, marriage and children, jobs, hobbies for their spare time, etc., but if you ask them, 'Are you happy, do you feel satisfied and fulfilled?' they answer that for all their activity, possessions and occupations, there is something lacking. What is it they lack? The zest, the taste that makes you savour life and feel happy and fulfilled, the subtle mysterious and elusive element that turns everything into joy no matter how dull and insignificant!

For example, a young man spends his entire time studying, working dutifully, his life has nothing particularly extraordinary or marvelous about it. But let this young man fall in love with a pretty girl, all of a sudden the world changes and everything sings to him, flowers, birds, the sun and stars! The world is the same but the new element in his life has transformed it into beauty and splendour. If the girl betrays him, if he becomes disillusioned, then once again the world will be drab and no matter how brightly the sun shines for others, to him it will be dark. Before, when he was in Paradise, no amount of rain, sleet, privation, insult or injury could dampen his spirits, it was all happiness and inspiration, poetry, music and wonderment... because he possessed the element that clothed his world in beauty.

The fact that love transforms the world is a well-known phenomenon, but no one bothers to draw conclusions. If it is true that love transforms life, might we not be able to experience this transforming feeling that makes everything beautiful without being in love with a man or woman? Of course it is possible. If love can alter your outlook and feelings, then perhaps there are other elements capable of doing that also. If you think the Initiates limit themselves to the kind of love that poets and artists seem to find so wonderful (in spite of the results), you are wrong. No, the Initiates, having explored this question thoroughly and carefully, discovered that true and lasting inspiration and fulfillment can only be obtained by going higher, much higher than ordinary men to the place where they can grasp the eternal element that never fades. Once the human heart and soul has this very subtle and imponderable element, everything takes on another, a universal, dimension. It requires work, prayer and meditation over a long period of time but once you capture it, everything is transformed.

Of course, love is one way of obtaining it. If you are in love with a lovely young girl, thanks to the way she inspires you, the element will be there, but it is not in her, nor is it in poetry or music. I have met many creative people who were as satisfied as they could be, but still, something was lacking! Anyone who succeeds in capturing this element on the summit of the universe will not lack anything, he will be able to triumph over all his difficulties.

Do not look for happiness or for the solution to your problems on the lower planes, the soul and spirit need an element that is not to be found on the lower planes. Go up to the heights and ask for it there, that is where you will find it.

Food and drink are all very well, but if you are not in good health, how will you enjoy them? Health gives savour to food, the slightest cold makes everything taste pale and insipid. Swimming pools, cars and money are all very well, but you must be in good health to appreciate them. So you see, the element of health changes your point of view toward many things. In the same way, if you have no love, no intelligence, then your possessions, your activity will bring you nothing but a shortlived material satisfaction.

Let us take love: when you love someone, the person is a genius, an angel as far as you are concerned; if you stop loving him, all at once he is a demon! You see, it all depends on whether the element love is in you or not in you... that one element changes everything. People think they are chemists, but they don't even know that spiritual chemistry exists, which is the answer to everything that happens to you. Chemists attribute these things to material elements, but it is the spiritual chemistry at the base, the origin of all phenomena that explains them. No one knows this spiritual chemistry that produces miracles in cases where the other chemistry fails. Yes, cases where an element called faith intervenes and miraculously heals someone... that is the important chemistry![1]

I say that health, love and light are elements that bring about great transformations; when they are not present, it is another kind of transformation that takes place. Another element beyond health, beyond love and light, exists that the others all depend on... an element that is part of God Himself. How do we obtain this element? Only through sacrifice, abnegation, self-denial.

I often tell you, you put the baby in the bathtub, but then instead of holding onto the baby and letting out the dirty water, you do the opposite, you hold on to the dirty water and throw out the baby! Symbolically speaking, the baby represents everything that is alive and divine and the water, everything that is dead, stagnant, polluted. People throw out the baby and keep the dirty water! You long to possess certain things... very good... but what about making sure that you have the element that will let you enjoy what you possess? So many wealthy people are sad and bored in spite of their wealth because they have lost the flavour: the joy of owning things is deadened by so much opulence. Everyone thinks possessions are the most important thing, but it is the sensation, the joy you feel because of them that is important. You may have a mansion filled with treasures but if you are dead, will you be able to enjoy them? You have to be alive to enjoy things! People are preoccupied with dead things; the more dead things they accumulate, the less alive they are and the less they rejoice!

Do you long for cars, money, a swimming pool, a lover or mistress? Well, make sure you are capable of enjoying them, that you have the sensitivity inside to rejoice over them. But no, all your time is spent looking for something more to possess. When you understand this truth, you will want to diminish the amount of things you own and increase the quality of your feelings. If you can do it, the little you have left will keep you in a permanent state of ecstasy! The lad who falls in love for the first time, anything the girl gives him, a rose petal, a little lock of hair, sends him into ecstasy! He may not have any money in the bank, no car, no job, but he is ecstatic because the girl he loves has given him something, he holds the rose petal in his hands, breathes its fragrance rapturously, puts it under his pillow at night and writes poems about it. Because of it he possesses the entire world. This is a psychological fact well worth noting; psychological facts are a good source of information.

Instead of running after physical pleasures and possessions, the disciple should try to intensify and embroider each spiritual joy he experiences, which will cultivate sensitivity... and then he will be able to spend centuries gazing at the stars, a rose, a face! There are so many things even here on earth that can plunge one into ecstasy, only the ability to feel is not vibrant anymore, people have lost the faculty of feeling deeply and only rejoice when they are indulging in physical pleasure. That appeals to them, but things that are beautiful, harmonious, musical and poetic, pure, mystic and divine, are of no interest. That is why they encounter so much disillusionment and sorrow.

'Take this, take that, and you will be happy!'say the advert-
isements on television, in newspapers and magazines, to make
people want a comfort and pleasure that will never give them
what they really need. The Initiates say, 'Climb, climb high in
prayer and meditation, to receive the subtle element that will
give you a taste for life.' This element is no more than a little
invisible atom but once you have it everything vibrates inside
you and life becomes beautiful. Without that element, even if
you own everything you ever wanted, you will feel empty and
disappointed.

And if you say, 'Ah, if only I could meet a great Master
and learn from him!' I will answer that you are not on the right
track, for unless you already have acquired the element that
will make it possible for you to appreciate a great Master and
love him as you should, even if he were the greatest Master on
earth, you would do nothing but argue and criticize and end up
as ignorant as ever.[2] Do not say, 'Well, if only I could marry a
marvelous girl!' or, 'If only I could discover where the Templars
hid their treasure!' for without the element I have been talking
about, the most beautiful girl in the world and all the gold in
the world will bring you nothing but misfortune.

That is the way you should think, dear brothers and sisters,
but you don't realize the value of what I tell you because you
are not used to thinking this way. Do you know, it would be
worth working for thousands of years to obtain this one element
that makes everything a cause for joy. As it is people trample
on things, sacred or not, splendid and precious or not, and
no matter how virtuous and qualified the person before them
is, no matter if they stand to gain the sun and the stars by
paying attention to him, they remain insensitive and nothing
can bring them out of their gloom and misery, they feel nothing,
understand nothing, and see none of the splendour around them.
That is the way humans are! And they consider it normal to
be that way. I repeat, even if Angels and Archangels came
down from Heaven and mingled with you, as long as you

have not worked on obtaining this element that knows how to recognize and appreciate the value of things, you will go on being unhappy wherever you go, even in Paradise you will not see the splendour of the Kingdom of God.

When I tell you that Heaven and earth can be yours, you do not believe me. It is true, the whole world can be yours. How? By belonging to you inwardly. Why must it be externally... what would you do with all those mountains and forests? I tell you that Heaven and earth will belong to me and to you also one day, but you do not understand. How could one thing be the property of so many? What belongs to one person cannot belong to another in the physical world, but in the divine world it is possible. An image: a rich man owns a beautiful garden full of magnificent trees and flowers, but he is so immersed in his business affairs that he has no time to walk in it or see its beauty. Along comes a poet and spends all his time in the garden listening to the birds, contemplating the flowers and fountains, breathing the fragrance of the roses and turning it all into poetry. Does the garden not belong to the poet? 'What about the owner?' you ask. The taxes belong to him! The earth is the property of a great many countries, but it belongs to me. Why not? And to you too. It is simply a question of adjustment.

I am giving you a secret today that will enable you to obtain anything you want. Go to the very highest point, grasp a tiny particle at the summit, absorb it, and you will feel that you own the world, you are Master of the world! Yes, that is how one feels. I am trying to lead you to realize the most subtle and wonderful sensations but if you think possessions are the ultimate solution, you never will. No, there is another element to work on, the taste that will let you enjoy things. Taste is in inverse proportion to quantity, the more you increase the material side, the more taste decreases. Take lovers, in the beginning, they exchange looks and smiles, write little notes to each other and feel that everything they do is heavenly. When

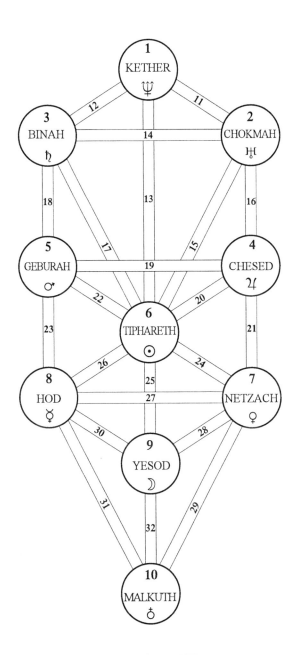

TREE OF LIFE

they go a little further, they no longer have the same joy and inspiration. The truth is that when you weigh down one side of the scales, the other side automatically becomes lighter. Never forget this, each time you augment something, stop and ask yourself what is decreasing at the same time. For instance, if you spend your time increasing your wealth, you might wonder if your health is not decreasing.

Take what I am giving you today and keep it in mind for the rest of your life. Stay on this path, keep on in the same direction, then everything will be beautiful, then you will be happy. A wife who tells her husband, 'Darling, how handsome you are! Never have I seen anyone so attractive!' is using the form of philosophy that transforms everything. But if you use the other, negative philosophy, you will have to grope around unhappily for a long time, believe me. Of course you won't be able to find the needed element right away, but the fact of reaching out for it already improves things, and you will be surprised to find yourself surrounded with Angels and Archangels and divinities. Only you must always keep going towards the top of the pyramid.

You ask, 'What is the element called?' It has no name, this subtle substance can only be found in the Sephira *Kether*[3] at the very top of the Tree of Life. Those who have found it were able to transform their bodies to the point of radiating light, projecting particles of light wherever they went. It is the explanation of the phenomenon of the Transfiguration, when Jesus appeared before three of his disciples shining with light. Although they were speechless with wonder and enraptured at what they saw, they had no idea what created the phenomenon:[4] it was this element.

The element is imponderable and extremely subtle but it is nevertheless matter. Few Initiates or Masters have ever reached *Kether*, few have ever obtained the element, for *Kether* is a world beyond dimension, beyond knowing, where the Heavenly Father, the Creator of all worlds, lives. Few have reached *Kether* because of the unbearable intensity of its vibrations, the rare beings who lived to return were able to do so only because of the special grace from Heaven which protects the physical body.

The *Book of Revelation* in which St. John describes his visions, reveals that he was one of the few to reach *Kether*. An Angel handed him a little book saying, *'Take it and eat it up, it shall make thy belly bitter, but it shall be in thy mouth sweet as honey.'* This little book found in the Sephira *Binah,* is the symbol of the element that preserves and protects the physical body. The Prophet Ezekiel also refers to a book given him by an Angel to eat. Another symbol of the same element was the burning coal placed on the mouth of Isaiah by the Seraphim.

Spiritual chemistry is the science of the elements used by God in creating the world, of which there are twenty-two. The first one, Aleph, has the power to transform, sublimate and enlighten; the last one, Tav, preserves and protects from destruction. Jesus said, *'I am Alpha and Omega,'* meaning, 'I have within me the two elements of the heavenly chemistry, one enabling me to sublimate everything, and the other permitting me to realize Heaven on earth.' There you have the meaning of Alpha and Omega, Aleph and Tav.

You must know how to climb all the way to the heights if you want to obtain the element in the Sephira *Kether*. Sometimes it comes down here to us, but most of us cannot receive it, we are closed up in ourselves, barricaded behind thick layers of darkness that prevent it from entering. *Yesod* is the only Sephira that opens our doors and windows to the element because of its purity. It is not necessary if you go through *Yesod* to make the tremendous effort (effort is often superfluous) to climb all the way to *Kether*, it is sufficient to wash oneself clean and transparent and pure so that the divine element can enter. When I say *climb*, it is not a question of going up or down, you can stay in place and open the path that leads from *Malkuth* to *Yesod*.

Between *Malkuth* where humans are and *Yesod* which is the
first station on the Tree of Life, the path is dark and mysterious,
filled with obstacles, it is a region that must be gone through by
the disciple if he wants to reach *Yesod*,[5] but it is fraught with
danger for it is where all the deceptions and aberrations and
deviations are. *Malkuth* is the region where we live, the Earth,
the world. The next station is *Yesod*, the region of the Moon.
If he wishes to arrive safely, the disciple must not attempt to
go from *Malkuth* to *Yesod* without being armed with advice
and instruction and light from his Master. He will have to face
temptation, suffer and lose his way, he will have setbacks, but if
his desire and will to succeed are unshakable, he will arrive.

Yesod, as I have explained, is divided into four regions,
as are the other Sephiroth. The lower part is a twilight region
one must go through as quickly as possible to attain the higher
regions which are filled with pure light. *Yesod* receives the
light and power and riches of all the Sephiroth, it has all the
virtues and qualities. The Sephiroth are like reservoirs filled to
overflowing and bubbling over impetuously with energy; it is
this energy that flows into *Yesod*. By drinking the pure waters
of *Yesod*, you absorb the virtues of all the Sephiroth at the
same time, you have only to purify yourself to receive them.
But unless you open yourself, they will turn round and round
outside you and not be able to enter.

If a windowpane is dirty you cannot see through it, even if
the sun is shining. In the past when there were only oil lamps,
the housekeeper had to clean them every day, otherwise the light
of the flame would not shine through. The same thing for man,
if he is not pure, his light is obscured and he will not see or
feel. As soon as he is pure, he becomes receptive to the cosmic
rays which fill him with beauty and riches of all kinds.

It says in the *Gospels*, *'Blessed are the pure in heart for
they shall see God.'* God is the plenitude, the abundance of the
Sephiroth, that is, the science, the understanding and penetration
of *Hod*; the fragrance, colours, beauty and celestial charm of

Netzach; the light and splendour of *Tiphareth;* the power and triumphant victory over inner and outer enemies of *Geburah;* the protection, justice, kindness and generosity of *Chesed;* the steadfastness and perseverance, the knowledge of Karma and destiny, of *Binah;* the eternal wisdom and beautiful harmony of *Chokmah;* the omnipotence of *Kether. Yesod* is the foundation, the condensation, the synthesis of all the virtues of all the Sephiroth and is called the foundation because purity is the foundation for all the rest.

Yesod is the pure life. You must decide to put purity first in your life, ahead of knowledge, wealth or power, it must be the basis for your existence. Today people are very knowledgeable and intelligent and learned, but they are not concerned with purity (what good does it do?) they are preoccupied with any number of things but because they lead impure lives, they fall ill or lose everything they possess... because the foundation was not solid. Yes, the foundation is the most important of all, dear brothers and sisters. Once we understand that and do all we can to acquire purity, then through the intermediary of *Yesod,* the qualities and virtues of all the Sephiroth will concretize and materialize themselves in *Malkuth,* the physical plane. There have been saints in the past who had no learning at all but worked exclusively on purity: all the other qualities including wisdom and clairvoyance and the power to heal came and manifested through them because there were no opaque layers, no thick screens to keep Heaven from entering. Purity brings health, knowledge, power, and joy. You don't know why, but you are full of joy!

Forget everything else if you wish, but remember the fact that purity is the basis for all the other acquisitions. The quintessence of the science of all the great founders of religion is the pure life.

Sèvres, 16th January, 1972

Notes

1. See *Love Greater Than Faith,* Izvor Coll. n° 239, chap. 4 : 'Your faith has made you well'.
2. See *What is a Spiritual Master ?,* Izvor Coll. n° 207, chap. 8 : 'The Disciple and His Master', and *Truth : Fruit of Wisdom and Love,* Izvor Coll. n° 234, chap. 4 : 'The Love of a Disciple ; the Wisdom of a Master'.
3. See *Angels and other Mysteries of The Tree of Life,* Izvor Coll. n° 236, chap. 2 : 'Introduction to the Sephirotic Tree of Life'.
4. See *'Et il me montra un fleuve d'eau de la vie',* Part IV, chap. 4 : 'L'édification du corps glorieux'.
5. Op. cit., Part X, chap. 1 : 'La porte du monde psychique: Iésod'.

Part II

PURITY

Chapter One

PURITY IS A QUESTION OF NOURISHMENT

In the few minutes we have left, dear brothers and sisters, perhaps some of you have a question you would like to ask that I could endeavour to answer...

Question: Master, would you please tell us how, in what way, we should think about purity.

Purity? There are many ways to consider purity, but perhaps the best way to start is to associate it with simplicity. Yes, purity is always uncomplicated, always clear and simple, that is, not a mixture of things that might go against its nature, impede its functioning or disturb its harmony. Let us take the human system. Why the human system? Because it isn't necessary to look only at the moral, ethical aspect of purity to understand it, purity belongs on every level, and the best way to start learning about it is to examine it on the physical plane, in the human system where it goes hand in hand with nutrition.

When it is a question of food, you eliminate the elements that do not contribute to your health or the wellbeing of your system, everything harmful or impure is removed. It may not look impure – poison can be transparent – but if you swallow it, you die. When you cut into a fruit, an orange or a tangerine for instance, it may look perfectly pure, but actually it is not, no food is ever entirely pure. What must the system do? The same as the nations do: place customs officers at the border to investigate your car and luggage (your food), and make sure nothing gets by (no illegal entry, no fraudulent importation of goods) that could harm the human system.

Unfortunately, man is generally in such a state that he obstructs the work of the customs officials. If you are anxious and worried, if you are tired and upset, you unconsciously impede the proper functioning of the little entities (your cells) whose duty is to survey everything as it appears, to sort out the edible and discard the poisonous. The way a man lives affects his cells, the way he thinks and feels and acts influences the little creatures that depend on him, they are affected when he behaves unreasonably, their sense of taste is deadened, they become corrupt and, in their greed and disorder and lack of discernment, they let in all kinds of poison and unwanted elements.

I have told you what a mistake it is for people to think that it is enough to have an outward semblance of courage, high morality, self-control, and then do anything they like when they are alone. It is when they are alone by themselves that people must set an example to their cells: the cells are children that must be brought up and educated properly,[1] they must have a good example before them to imitate. People do not realize their responsibility, in front of others they seem irreproachable but when they are face to face with themselves, they do whatever occurs to them, things that are not always strictly orthodox. The cells who are there watching and recording everything say to themselves, 'Well, if he can do that, we can get away with anything we wish!' And nothing will make them obey after that. I will not go over this subject again, I only want to make it clear that by not watching and surveying himself, man hinders the cells working to protect his organism, with the result that a tumor, fever, or illness will one day be able to enter unchallenged.

Purity brings health to the physical body, to the heart it brings happiness and joy, to the will it brings the power to act, to the mind it brings light and understanding. I wish I had more time to go into details about why purity is the root, the foundation for all the other virtues, even beauty. You are beautiful if you are pure, because once the screens and thick layers that prevent the light from showing through have been removed, your face shines with light. *Yesod* is the ninth Sephira on the Tree of Life (in Hebrew *Yesod* means foundation, base), where the Moon is also and the Moon rules over purity.

I hope you will excuse this rather hasty, haphazard way of answering this question but I cannot go into it more fully at the moment... I thought it would be a question that would take less time to answer. Purity is a profound subject, a most essential subject. I have always meditated on purity because I realized very early in life that without it everything else is useless. Each little impurity that gets into our bloodstream, our stomach, our thoughts and feelings, is the point of departure for all kinds of trouble in the future. You must think about purity all the time and meditate on it daily if you wish to have the advantages of the pure life.

Purity is not easy to find. As everyone knows, the air we breathe is poisoned by the odour of smoke and gas, our food and drink are poisoned by chemical products etc., etc. But what about other things such as the things we say and think and feel and desire... are they pure? You say, 'I thought the earth was supposed to absorb impurity and transform it.' Yes, it does, but not everything; it absorbs physical elements such as waste matter, but not impure thoughts and feelings. If you were sensitive enough to see and feel what is emitted by human beings, you would not be able to stand what they do, what they think about and long for...[2] their thoughts and feelings and desires are a poisonous mixture that their soul cannot absorb. What makes a diamond pure? The fact that it contains no mixture, nothing but pure carbon.

Purity is on every level. Pureness of the blood is the great secret of health for the physical body. The blood takes what it receives, good or bad, and distributes it throughout the system: if it is pure, the system enjoys good health. The first thing for a disciple is to purify his blood through nutrition and respiration, but it is just as important for him to survey his thoughts and feelings, to make sure they are pure before allowing them into his psychic being. Our thoughts and emotions must also be fed properly, for when we consume impure thoughts and feelings, we introduce into our system as much impurity as if we ate poisoned food. The laws are the same.

Yes, dear brothers and sisters, purity is not a matter of abstaining from sleeping with someone or other. There are boys and girls who have never been kissed whose hearts are full of desires and whose minds are full of thoughts that are indescribably filthy... and there are mothers with flocks of children, who are as pure as crystal. Sexual purity is tremendously important, but I mean by purity, purity of thought and feeling, that is where licentiousness and peculiar cravings are born. A person's inner state is responsible for his sexual behaviour on the physical plane.

I wish I had more time, things come to me that I would like to say, but be patient and wait, we will return to this subject later and you will see how rich and profound the world of purity is.

The Bonfin, 24th August, 1966

Notes
1. See *Cosmic Moral Law*, Complete Works, vol. 12, chap. 19: 'Example: the Best Method of Pedagogy ».
2. See *The Powers of Thought*, Izvor Coll. n° 224, chap. 3: 'Psychic Pollution'.

Chapter Two

SORTING AND SELECTING

Yesterday, we saw that one way to understand purity is to observe the way nutrition affects the human system. Today, we will see if there is anything else to be drawn from this idea.

In ancient days, human beings had no knowledge of hygiene as far as food was concerned, they ate like animals without cleaning or skinning their meat, fruit or vegetables, and they drank polluted water, etc., no one knew then about germs (a recent discovery!) and men swallowed everything whole the way beasts and birds of prey do. A cat spends time washing itself, but then it swallows a mouse whole, skin, bones, guts, whiskers and all! Man has progressed in this way, he knows that before swallowing fish, fruit, oysters, snails, and so on, he must remove the noxious part, the skin, pits, seeds, bones or shells, he must make a selection. On the surface, everyone knows how to eat, they never fail to remove the crust from a piece of cheese... and thus pass for highly civilized people!

But there are still countries in Asia or Africa, for instance, where hygiene is not widespread. When I was in India, I saw things that were far from sanitary (or appetizing) such as rats running around the hotel kitchens, and, on the Isle of Elephanta not far from Bombay, I saw people drinking stagnant water that was practically green! It seems it was a sacred shrine, but water is not sacred to bacteria. However these are particular cases and we should not dwell on them. On the whole, humans have made great progress in the way they eat, they know about sterilizing, refining, pasteurizing, etc., and accept the fact that a sorting must be made in order to eliminate indigestible or harmful elements.

The act of separating and rejecting part of what he eats places man on a level above the animals, but he needs to understand that he consumes another kind of food that must also be cleaned, washed, purified. The good must be separated from the bad, the pure from the impure in his thoughts and feelings that are also food for the human system. Man must progress a little further and learn to sort his psychic food as carefully as he sorts his physical food; for the moment, he is like the cat that swallows everything whether it is edible or not.

In the Emerald Tablet it says, 'separate the earth from the fine, the subtle from the gross...' that is, the pure from the impure. Hermes Trismegistus was speaking of the philosopher's stone, but it is the same principle. The pure must be separated from the impure as gold and precious stones are separated from the matrix, the rock and earth that envelops them. All life is a system of sorting and discarding, in industries and business, trades and professions, shops, groceries, diamonds and precious stones, competitions and examinations, there is always the need to eliminate, even when picking a general or Miss World! Why do we not realize that we must do the same sorting and elimination in the world of our inner lives? Ask anyone, even the most learned men, what are the thoughts and feelings which cause men to fall ill and disintegrate... they are unaware of the difference and think that thoughts and feelings are all the same. What they must learn is that in the field of the mind and heart, there is as much sorting to be done between good and bad quality as there is for food (grade A, grade B, etc.)

The materials used in the past for heating and lighting were made of such inferior quality that the smoke hurt the eyes and the smell was almost asphyxiating! Nowadays, with electricity, there is no residue, no smoke fumes and even when coal is used, there are several grades available, from the kind that gives a lot of heat and leaves no slag or débris to the kind that gives very little heat and leaves a great deal of residue. All combustible matter, coal, wood, gas, oil, straw, has a few non-combustible elements, but in different proportions, and that is the important thing to remember: all material is either excellent or inferior, there is always a choice to be made, and it is the same for feelings.

Feelings are like combustibles, not all are top quality, not all give the best light or heat or action. As with food there are feelings that can be ingested as they are, and others that must be discarded because dirt or slag or germs have crept in which must be removed before the astral stomach can digest them. If you are in the grip of hatred or jealousy, if you have a craving for revenge, what happens? There will be plenty of heat perhaps, but with it a lot of smoke, an odour of putrefaction, a residue that will poison you. And this humans do not know. Official science offers no possibility of studying feelings in detail and classifying them before filing them away. We believe in expressing our feelings no matter what, we eat them, we feast on them without a thought for the consequences. We do the same with our thoughts, they are never sorted, none are discarded, there is no scale, no set of values for thoughts.

Anyone who thinks he can freely express his passions and desires no matter how depraved and degenerate they may be, shows that he doesn't know the human structure, he has not studied the way man was created originally in the workshops of the Lord. It is enough for him that his stomach or sex demand satisfaction. Very well, but what about some sort of selection? Young people will cry, 'No, no, no selectivity.' They select their food with all the care in the world, but they see no danger in

allowing themselves every feeling that comes along and all
the pleasure they can find at all costs. It is the same as being
poisoned by food. They don't mind whom they kiss or sleep
with, because they don't know that some people carry around
nauseating elements in themselves, clouds of filthy emanations
which they then absorb exactly as if they were wading around in
the sewer. I am not against making exchanges, but one should
know how to make them in order not to become contaminated.
This is a subject for reflection.

Exchanges between people should have a beautifying,
improving effect, resulting in mutual amelioration, not a
deterioration. Love should be a source of enrichment for both
partners, not something that leaves them ill or emotionally
unbalanced from having swallowed too many irregular elements.
The point is not to refuse love, but to make a choice and accept
only love that is pure and luminous... in order to become pure
and luminous yourself. A boy and girl entwined together are not
aware that an osmosis takes place between them. Yes, from the
electromagnetic aspect, there is an osmosis of their emanations
and this will have all kinds of repercussions: the weaknesses
and faults of the boy will penetrate the girl, and vice versa. And
the same for qualities.

Love creates a levelling between two people, and that is why
it is best to apply the law of sorting and grading to the quality
of your feelings before undergoing this levelling. The law
applies to love as it applies to food, your astral intake should
be examined as carefully as your physical food, to see where
it comes from, what it contains, what you will absorb, etc.
Unfortunately young people do not like to pause and consider,
and very rarely does their intuition come to their aid and tell
them what to do (or what not to do) for their future happiness.
In spite of all their education and learning, they are not guided
by wisdom in these cases, but by their feelings. I am not against
feelings, I have never denied the need for love... on the contrary,
it is the whole meaning of life, but I say that young people

should acquire discernment, they should learn to discern and discriminate, and to choose the best.

Just as there is variety in the food you eat (bread, fruit, vegetables, fish or meat, etc.), so in the realm of feelings there is variety: some feelings are delicatessen food, yes, sausages and ham, and some are fruit or wine, but as man knows nothing about the world of feelings, he eats anything that comes along, and then he falls ill. He must learn not to let in the things that poison him such as anger, wickedness, cruelty, jealousy, and... especially sensuality, the form of love that contains the most harmful elements.

People talk about love without knowing what constitutes real love. A proof for you: a man loves a woman, he is burning with love, and in this he is entirely sincere, however, his love is the same as that of an animal, a savage beast, he is hungry and he wants to eat. Does he think about her happiness? No, he is thinking about himself, he is hungry and he helps himself, what happens to her is of no importance to him and when he has finished devouring her, he will go and find someone else. Love can be far from pure and noble, but everyone still calls it love! Another man loves a woman, but thinks only about her future wellbeing, her health and beauty, her elevation, all he wants is to protect her and see that she is happy. Both attitudes are called 'loving,' but what a difference between them! Real love makes you love others uniquely for the sake of helping them evolve. To kiss someone is easy, but to express love for them after many years is another matter. The evidence of love is a kiss, an evidence that must continue to be expressed over a long period of time, whereas most of the time, it is forgotten a few days later.

The world is full of people boiling over with desire, that is what is most prevalent in the world now, but the thing that is practically non-existent is wisdom, the wisdom that insists on choosing. It is the rarest, most precious thing, but no one ever seeks it, no one wants it. Why? Because humans do not reason correctly. They say, 'Wisdom would mean giving up a joy, renouncing a pleasure that we do not wish to renounce.' Which shows how ignorant they are, for they would be far happier if they had the wisdom to discern between feelings. When you can't see, when you do nothing to protect yourself, you are at everyone's mercy. Don't think that you can be happy if you are blind! It is as though you put your hand in a paper bag without looking: there is a snake that will bite you.

Man has several other bodies beside his physical body: the etheric, astral, mental, causal, Buddhic and Atmic bodies.[1] By giving free rein to his passions, he stirs up the currents on the astral plane and attracts monstrous entities from that region who then invade mankind through him. This ignorance on the part of man concerning his own structure and the fact that he is constantly making exchanges with invisible beings from the other regions of the universe, are the cause of his misfortunes. The disciple knows how he is constructed and is aware of his close relationship with the inhabitants on the other planes, he is conscious of the need to sort and select the elements he eats, to close the door to hostile forces and open them only to beneficial, harmonious and constructive ones.

My dear brothers and sisters, your body is made of the materials you absorb, if they are pure, you will be pure, but if they are not pure, eventually you will be ill. This is the law on the physical plane, and it is also the law on the psychic plane. In the same way that your food must be cleaned and washed before it is eaten, so your thoughts and feelings must be surveyed night and day to guard against the poisonous ones. Are there customs officers at the border of your country to keep out any dangerous or illegal entry? No, anyone can come in from no matter where and poison you. Place inspectors at the borderline and stop each thought as it presents itself, 'One minute, please. Where have you come from? What are your colours? If I let you in, what will you bring in with you?' In that way you can prevent catastrophic results from certain thoughts that visit you. But that is not what you do, you analyse nothing, you swallow angry thoughts of revenge and think, 'Ah, I'll get him!' But what will you get?

Most people accept no matter what in the way of feelings, no matter what in the way of ideas (political for instance), without reflecting or discriminating, which is why as far as Initiates are concerned they are like the cat that swallows the mouse whole. They bathe several times a day but do they wash themselves inwardly? The dirt accumulates, mountains of dirt! Carefully dressed and outwardly presentable, on the inside they consume appalling thoughts that spread dreadful emanations everywhere around them. Why don't they wash them away? Once again, it is because they are ignorant. Sometime I will tell you how to wash and cleanse yourselves so as to get rid of the inner dirt.

Bodies are formed by the elements we absorb, therefore, whether it is for the physical body, the etheric, astral, or mental bodies, what we consume must be carefully sorted, nothing must be accepted that is dirty or rotten or harmful in some way. Sorting is a science! Thoughts and feelings are not made of the same material, quality exists for them also, and the higher you go to seek the materials they are made of, the purer they will be. On the physical plane, what is pure and light rises to the top, and what is impure and heavy, the dregs, the slag and silt, sink to the bottom. And the purer the material, the more resistant it is... construct your body with the purest materials and you will be able to resist illness and pain and even death, for the quality of your substance will be such that neither pain nor death can get a grip on you. Illness and death have power only if they can hold on, the Devil himself is powerless unless he can find a weakness or vice, some impurity to hold onto. If we are faced with all kinds of unpleasant things in life, it is because we allowed the forces of evil to fasten on to us and get inside.

As I am always telling you, I am not in favour of reading books in which I find none of the great truths of life. In the Living Book of Nature, Cosmic Intelligence has inscribed everything we should know. For instance, what I told you today I discovered from insects, ants and cockroaches and bugs. Insects do not enter a clean house, but if you leave a little dirt, a bit of decayed food around, they all gather. How do they know it is there? And why do fleas and bedbugs bite certain people and not others? Because the blood contains impure ingredients that attract them: they feed on filth. If you want to avoid insects, keep your house clean; if you want to avoid being stung, keep your blood pure!

What I want to be sure you understand is that the same phenomenon exists on the psychic plane. In the *Gospels* it says that demons take possession of certain people... why? Because they find impure things to feed on, and that is what they seek.[2] Incense in churches and temples purifies and chases away demons (which are attracted by nauseating odours). That is why sorcerers use evil smells: to invoke demons, along with bats and owls and rats and snakes.

Thus Cosmic Intelligence shows us that if we let impurities penetrate on the physical plane, we open the door to germs and microbes, and if we let impurities in on the astral and mental planes, we open the door to demons. Jesus, after chasing the demons out and healing a person, always said to him, *'Go and sin no more!'* that is, do not let impurities in anymore. Does anyone take this seriously nowadays? Do young people realize that by absorbing impure fluids on the astral plane, they are opening the door to anomalies of all kinds? They must learn this, for the correspondence is absolute. As essential as it is for man's health, beauty and intelligence to sort and select his physical nourishment, so is it equally essential to be careful with his spiritual nourishment: his future depends on it. The quality of the elements will make him sickly and weak and decrepit, or strong and beautiful and expressive. The same law exists on the physical plane and on the astral and mental planes.

You ask, 'But how is it possible to select thoughts and feelings, and how do we know whether they are pure or impure?' It is simple: thoughts and feelings that are personal and selfish are impregnated with elements from the world below, and cannot be pure; thoughts and feelings that have to do with our own interests, our own profit or success or advantage, and do nothing useful or good for the rest of the world, are impure; greed, jealousy, anger, sensuality, etc., are impure. Whereas feelings such as abnegation, unselfishness, sacrifice, patience, generosity, kindness and gentleness, love, the desire to be one with God in order to bring light to others and do useful and beneficial things for the world... those are pure.

Now you have a criterion to go by. If your life is full of personal desires, rancour, jealousy and scandalmongering, you may think you are pure but in reality you are not. You may be clothed in satin and velvet and jewels, but any clairvoyant would see that in the astral world you are surrounded by dark and disgusting colours, each one corresponding to a vice or weakness. Fine, elevated feelings, on the other hand, fill you with particles of such purity that you appear on the astral or Buddhic planes surrounded by clear and sparkling, iridescent and beautiful colours that dazzle the beholder. The clairvoyant who recognises the connection between colours and virtues, will distinguish your colours, the colour of your faith, the colour of your love, the colour of your patience, etc.

I do not believe someone who thinks he is pure simply because he has never embraced a woman. My God, if that was all! What about his desires and thoughts and feelings, what about the dreadful colours that float around him? The correspondence between colours and virtues (or vice) is a whole science, handed down by thousands of Initiates and clairvoyants throughout the ages; it is valid eternally, nothing can alter the truth.

I have mainly stressed the importance of feelings in this little talk, but it is the same hierarchy in the world of thoughts. Thoughts that are entirely personal, scheming and egotistical, emanate drab and repulsive colours that reveal to those who can see, how clever that person is at cheating, at pushing others aside, at destroying them for his own profit. Initiates on the other hand, allow themselves only the best thoughts, they concentrate on the light and on the wellbeing of all living creatures all over the earth, on the Kingdom of God, on becoming one with Cosmic Intelligence and climbing up to the summit, on reaching the light... and their mental body shines with the colours of holiness, more beautiful than the astral colours. Saints are always depicted with a golden halo above their heads, but they have the other colours also, violet, heavenly blue, emerald green. In the aura of an Initiate there are many shades and nuances besides the colours of the prism, and their beauty is indescribable.[3]

That is why I say to you, dear brothers and sisters, that if you concentrate on a great Initiate of the past, or if you have the tremendous privilege of being near a Master who is alive and living here on earth, who has worked for centuries and millenniums on purity and filled his being with heavenly particles which he radiates on those around him in order to purify and benefit them... I say, if you can concentrate on him, if you contemplate such a being as that, you will become pure yourself.[4]

The best method of purification is to be near as constantly as possible to someone who has already achieved purity in all his bodies, physical, astral and mental, and who refuses to entertain the thoughts, desires and passions that might drag others down or prevent them from getting out of their state of gloom and sadness, someone who knows that each thought and feeling he has is reflected on those around him. You see how much it takes to be an Initiate! At all times he must be vigilant, even when he sleeps he must be conscious. Yes, he knows that he is at the head of the rope that binds all the others to him and, if he makes one false step, they will all go into the precipice. But disciples are not concerned with the worries their Master might have, they are too preoccupied with their own little affairs to see what goes on in his soul and spirit. He can only wait until they understand that he wants to bring them the purest and the most luminous things that exist. But let us leave all that for now.

From today's talk retain simply this: purity and impurity are both the result of the quality and quantity of the food you absorb on each one of the planes. As you eat your food, you absorb part of it and reject another part, the dregs.

When you overeat, your system is unable to take care of all the waste matter, and you must eliminate frequently... people who let themselves overindulge in passions also must eliminate more frequently.[5]

You say: 'But I have a right to all the desires and sensations I like!' Very well, but then your astral stomach will be overburdened, you will have a great deal of waste matter to get rid of and, as there is no place set aside for such things in the astral world, you will be forced to turn to those around you: a man who overeats on the astral plane will have to find a woman to rid himself of the overflow, and vice versa. Animals, who have no special place set aside for excrement, leave their dirt anywhere without bothering; men with gross astral desires behave the way animals do on the physical plane. When you overindulge on the intellectual plane by reading anything and everything and mixing too many subjects, you overtax your brain, which is the reason there are so many nervous and psychic disorders in the world. It is dangerous to overeat on any of the planes.

My dear brothers and sisters, nutrition is the point of departure, the key, to your understanding of the laws on the different planes of your being, your life.

The Bonfin, 25th August, 1966

Notes

1. See *'You Are Gods'*, Synopsis Coll., Part II 'What is human nature?', and *'Et il me montra un fleuve d'eau de la vie'*, Synopsis Coll., Part III: 'L'homme dans l'Arbre de vie'.
2. See *Life Force*, Complete Works, vol. 5, chap. 7: 'Unwanted Guests'.
3. See *Man's Subtle Bodies and Centres – the Aura, the Solar Plexus, the Chakras...*, Izvor Coll. n° 219, chap. 2: 'The Aura'.
4. See *What is a Spiritual Master?*, Izvor Coll. n° 207, chap. 10: 'The Magical Presence of a Master'.
5. See *The Yoga of Nutrition*, Izvor Coll. n° 204, chap. 4: 'Choosing Your Food', chap. 5: 'Vegetarianism', chap. 6: 'The Ethics of Eating'.

Chapter Three

PURITY AND THE SPIRITUAL LIFE

This morning on the Rocher, dear brothers and sisters, we beheld purity! And what splendour! Purity was everywhere, in the air, in the colours of the sky, it was so clear that the horizon vibrated. This is the kind of morning when, if you know how to look at colours and communicate with the dawn, the sun, the sky, you become pure yourself.

If you need an explanation for the word purity, it will not be easy... to understand intellectually is one thing, but to understand in one's soul intuitively, is another. If I explain intellectually what purity is, there will be misunderstanding. People see things differently because of their different needs and tastes: if something pleases them, they think it is pure. There are lovers who justify their taste for the sensual and depraved on the grounds that they are expressing love! To them love purifies everything... and are they sincere? Yes, surely. And so, how does one distinguish pure from impure...

Two thieves went into a church to steal. They climbed on a chair with the intention of taking down one of the chandeliers, but as the chair was not high enough, one of them fetched a table. The table not being high enough either, he fetched a huge Bible, placed it on the table, and stood on it. The other was indignant. 'What are you doing, you wretch? That is the Bible you are standing on!' 'Oh,' said the other. 'When your heart is pure, what difference does it make?' His heart was so pure that he could steal a chandelier, stand on the Bible, or anything else! Many people justify themselves that way.

When new brothers and sisters first arrive at the Brotherhood, I am always interested to see what tendencies they have developed. Some lead a vegetable life, they eat and drink and live, of course, but in a way that is similar to the plants: they work, they move around a little, but inside there is no life, no inner life, their entire life is taken up with eating, drinking, sleeping, and doing the minimum of work: a vegetative life. Others have a predominantly animal tendency, they are more animated, indeed they buzz with impulses, instincts, passions and desires! And other people are more emotional, they have a more highly developed imagination and a poetic, musical tendency, but no philosophy, no divine ideal. Another category has a highly developed intellect, they like to study, they are the writers, the thinkers, the philosophers who learn everything. But the mind, the intellect, is limited! Less so than in the instinctive, vegetative or emotional people, but still intellectuals are not in possession of the true light.

Above and beyond the activity of the mind is the activity of the spirit that makes it possible for man to have the essential element that none of the other activities give him. The spiritual life carries with it an abundance, a fulfillment that our contemporaries will never know, because they are limited by their intellect. In the past, people didn't count so much on education, now everyone wants to be intellectual and belong to the intelligentsia. That there might be other, higher aims, that Cosmic Intelligence might have foreseen other advantages for humans and is trying to make them explore regions that are far richer and more rewarding than the mental region... that they do not see. To them, the intellectual level is a source of pride, the last word... if they knew how wrong they are![1]

It makes me sad to see people who have developed one side only, the instinctive or vegetative or intellectual side, because I know they will not lead useful lives, they will eat and drink and bring children into the world, but they will never be affected by the spiritual side of life, all the richness and beauty and splendour of the universe will not be noticed by them. Why limit oneself to the visible and tangible and material, why not accept a new element, why not believe in something new?

To live the spiritual life means to push back the horizon and give the soul immense possibilities, but people are afraid they will be depriving themselves of something, their appetites and tendencies and projects are ordinary and prosaic, but the thought of giving them up is upsetting. All I say is that those people are not enlightened, they don't realize that their freedom and happiness and entire future depend on the acquisition of a spiritual life. They should be thinking, 'Yes, it's true, we have certain weaknesses and desires and passions that are disquieting to say the least, which we would like to try and curb even if they can't be made to disappear completely, so as to find out about the higher world of the spirit and be able to taste some of its joys... perhaps they will be finer and subtler than anything we ever tasted!' But that is not the way people reason, they hold on to the same old attitude even in an Initiatic School, even if they were let into the Temple of the Highest Mysteries, they would have that attitude. They are closed and set in their ways, they eat, drink, listen, participate in our work, in exercises, but, consciously or unconsciously, they refuse to open themselves, they are shut off inwardly and do not vibrate with us. How do I know? For me it is quite simple, I have only to look at someone to know how he thinks, whether he is open or closed, whether he seeks the spiritual life or something quite different. You say, 'If that is not what they are looking for, why do they come?' They come because of intellectual curiosity perhaps, or to please their parents, or the friends that brought them. But within themselves they are locked up tight, rigid and tense, and as far as they are concerned, they will make no effort.

If they knew what they miss by closing themselves off from the divine life, if they knew that they are prolonging the pain and disillusion and uncertainty of their lives that way, if they knew that they are facing illness and trouble of all kinds... not only because of their attitude here, but everything they do shows that they have turned their backs on the spirit. Hurrah for ignorance! Hurrah for whatever keeps us ignorant and forever limited by materialism!... Nothing can be better than the way we are! People hold on to ignorance, believe me, even if it means being trampled on and ground to bits, people hold on to ignorance. Where would they be without it?

What am I supposed to think when I see such narrow-mindedness, such unwillingness to make any effort to penetrate the higher world of the spiritual life? Well, let them go on leading their lives of eating, drinking, having many children and houses and cars and money. The ending to that fairy tale is that they will *not* live happily ever after. My analysis is exact, you will see. Even if you do not understand it now, you will one day see that I am telling you the truth, and you will regret not having accepted to work spiritually.

Many of you are unconsciously closed to the spiritual life without really meaning to be, but because of heredity or education, or because you never analysed yourself and don't realize what you are like, you have a scorn for everything sacred. Observe yourselves! Become conscious of the fact that you are closed inside and do something about it! Otherwise you will go on for years and years without ever being impressed by anything new, without ever making a real discovery, without experiencing any enlightenment or revelation. If you really wish to advance, you must open yourselves.

The spiritual world is so near, near enough for us to reach out and touch! Yes, the physical and spiritual worlds are adjacent, touching each other... one might say that man is the heart of the invisible world; if he cannot feel this, it is because the thoughts and feelings he has brought with him from the past are too dark, too dense, nothing can penetrate, no fusion or contact can take place.

Listen to what I am saying, dear brothers and sisters, for these are things you should know. We are always talking about the spiritual life and mystical, divine things (we talk too much in fact), but do we realize the great advantages, the great riches the spiritual life offers us? No, we do not believe it, we do not feel it. Very few dare to launch out into spirituality. The rest are afraid, afraid of being ridiculed, diminished or weakened in some way, robbed of their customary joys and pleasures. That is not so, nothing is lost. The spiritual world, when it is understood and lived properly, strengthens, enriches, beautifies and reinforces our lives. We have inherited notions that do not correspond with reality and it is time we replaced them.

If you attempt to dissuade me by saying that all the religious mystics you know of led lives of privation, suffering and torment, and comported themselves in peculiar ways... I will answer that you mistake something that was not spiritual for real spirituality, or in any case something that was not a true manifestation of it. Examples of true spirituality are not to be found amongst mentally unbalanced people with mystical or mediumistic tendencies. The spiritual life is an exact and precise science, not a vague groping around in the dark. But be patient, you will be given all the criteria you need to keep you from going wrong on this subject.

Some people are afraid of spirituality because they have never been shown what it is, others imagine it consists in going to church to light candles and confess to the priest, give a few pennies to the poor, recite the psalms and listen to the Gospel. No, true spirituality is a quality of life, it means living ahead of time a heavenly life, perfectly pure and harmonious. To live the spiritual life constantly and without cease is to have a real contact, a profound relationship with Heaven itself... not merely to do things externally, a gesture, a posture of devotion. 'Spiritual' means manifestation of the spirit. Too often it is the form that takes precedence over a sincere striving to contact the sublime life.[2] One meets so-called pious spiritualists who have everything *except* the spirit, the spirit is absent. If you have the spirit, you have a new life that flows from you and purifies and vivifies and ressuscitates everything around you. It may not be you, you may never do or say anything, but the spirit manifests itself through you. How? That is the miracle. You may also be on your knees for years and light candles night and day, without the spirit ever coming to visit you.

The time is coming when everyone will know what true spirituality is because we will all be living it uninterruptedly. How much spirituality can there be in someone with a dark dull face, a sinister expression and hollow eyes? What spirituality can there be if there is no light or love? The spiritual life is full of love, abnegation, sacrifice, kindness, and gentleness. There have been people who thought it was being spiritual to be intransigent, implacable and cruel, to them being spiritual meant being fanatical and condemning other people to the stake. One day there will be nothing left of those concepts.

In India and Japan there are monks and yogis who spend their time doing extremely difficult exercises to develop their willpower, but they never think of studying themselves, they don't analyze the results of what they do to see if there is something other than transformation that takes place at that time. They have closed, frozen faces, they are distant and hard with others. Perhaps that is the way to become an ascetic, but asceticism is not yet spirituality. It is not necessary to destroy your love, warmth, gentleness and kindness in order to develop your will, the two can go hand in hand. You cannot develop spirituality by developing one thing only, whether it is your will, your mind or your heart. True spirituality includes the light of the mind, the warmth of the heart, and something else: the life of the spirit.

People who deprive themselves of the life of the spirit, preferring to stay away because they are afraid of not being like everyone else, or because they would rather believe in scientists, deprive themselves of all the wealth the spirit brings with it. They may have other things, worldly position, fame, wealth, but no more. The spirit brings plenitude, a man who is open to the spirit can overcome everything, conquer everything, and become a complete being.

People who have no interest in the spiritual life do not want to know where their real interests lie. I say to them, 'You poor wretched beings, you don't know what you are deprived of!' 'Maybe so,' they answer. 'But what does the spiritual life do for anyone?' The others may have the same difficulties and ups and downs to face, the same insects, that is, the same hardships, but the difference is, they know what to do, how to understand these difficulties and surmount them, and especially, how to use these very difficulties as a way of enriching themselves spiritually. Certain things are impossible to avoid on earth, cold, heat, hornets and mosquitoes, snakes, and humans who are cruel and unjust, but people who live the spiritual life have another point of view that offers them the possibility of being triumphant where others succumb.[3]

It is now twenty-nine years that you have been listening to me, and yet I see that not one of you really understands the advantages of the spiritual life. For one reason or another, you try to live it without understanding how much it has to offer. The day you do finally understand that, this life will be the only thing that counts for you, only then will everything you do, even the most insignificant ordinary things, take on a flavour, a taste that was not there before. The life of the spirit shows you the true meaning of things; and whether you are eating or drinking or walking, getting married, building houses or tearing them down, everything will have an extraordinary flavour for you because the essential is there, endowing each thing with value and beauty. Without that, everything will eventually lose its flavour.

Philosophers, scholars and scientists have misled generations of people by scorning spirituality and glorifying one thing only, the human mind. They have done incalculable harm, and they will be held responsible. Many scientists, writers, thinkers have ruined everything by their blind reasoning, their insistence on basing themselves and their opinions on the appearance of things only, that is, the dead side of Nature, and suppressing everything alive, profound, sacred and divine. They are wrong, they are in error, and life will teach them a lesson.[4] The invisible world is preparing certain events that will show them beyond a doubt that they must review their thinking. The time is coming when values as we know them will all be replaced.

Now, I will tell you something that is most important: the spiritual life makes all the cells, all the particles of your being vibrate and radiate; you emanate such luminous, magnetic, musical and fragrant waves that everyone begins to love you and to listen to you. When you have no spiritual life, you are drab and sombre, you lose your radiance and magnetism to such a degree that people do not even notice you and relegate you to a corner somewhere. 'No one loves me, no one pays any attention to me!' you complain. Have you done anything to be loved? Not if you have closed yourself off from the source of love that should always be flowing in order to nourish others.

The worst thing anyone can do is to close himself off from the spiritual life. One day the medical world will discover that mental and nervous illnesses come from the absence of a spiritual life, a spiritual goal, a spiritual ideal. And the same for spiritual galvanoplastics, that is, the work a mother does on her child during pregnancy to insure his perfect health mentally and physically, so that he will grow up to be noble, good, kind, intelligent and able. A few years ago, biologists discovered by studying mice that the condition of the mother mouse exerted a tremendous influence on her progeniture *before birth*. A brilliant discovery, a little late in coming![5]

People with no sense of observation, intellectual prowess or memory, but with a great love for the spiritual life, who have devoted themselves to it and nourished themselves with it for years and years, can change so much that their intelligence and understanding surpass that of the greatest intellectuals! Yes, if you love the spiritual life, if you let it enter and take over, it is capable of awakening extraordinary faculties in you. It takes time and patience, but the spiritual life can endow people with almost supernatural ability, I have seen examples of this. There are also scientists and learned men who have become intellectually sterile, because of their refusal to renew themselves at the source, the fountain of the spiritual life. Poor ignoramuses! The spiritual life should be the crown of all their activity. One day I will back the scientists into a corner with irrefutable arguments that Nature has distributed everywhere, and they will not be able to contradict. One thing only can save them: recognition of the fact that they failed to notice the proofs in front of their eyes.

People who have extraordinary qualities but not the spiritual ones, such as respect for others, understanding, kindness, nobleness, unselfishness, high-mindedness, are those people loved, do people seek them out? No, they are feared, they are bowed down to, they are submitted to, but they are not loved. To them I say, 'O you wise and learned people, how will you solve this problem?' They are not loved because they do not possess the elements of the spiritual life that awaken love, such as gratitude, enthusiasm, wonder, hope. Eliminate those elements and life becomes unbearable.

I was very young when I discovered the fact that if one wanted power, one should never seek it. Real power is not in commanding others, hitting them, punishing them, killing them... real power is to warm them, to pour so much warmth on them that they perspire with heat and have to remove all their clothes because of the heat. That is real power. Only the sun possesses it! He says, 'Ah, stand up to me, eh? I told you to take your overcoat off!' 'But I don't wish to.' 'You don't wish to? We'll see about that!' The sun begins to warm you and it is the sun who triumphs, for in no time you stand there before him completely naked! But this is a language you do not understand. I mean that if you want people to shed their misery, weaknesses and shortcomings, their illness and cruelty and wickedness, the only way is to heat them, warm them with love, it is the only way. If you hit someone or try to force him, he will retaliate. In any case he will be obstinate. You are obstinate, he is obstinate... and what then?

I am curious to see what those who spurn the spiritual life will be like in a few years... I already know the difficulties they will have to face. Nor does anyone explain to children that the spiritual life is the most necessary, the richest and most beautiful, and they too reject it. They want to become scientists and philosophers and leaders, but spirituality... what good is that? Religion bothers people, which is why it is in the process of disappearing.

To come back to purity (although I have talked about nothing but purity since I began), if you are at the mouth of a river, you see how dirty and full it is of all kinds of foreign matter. But if you climb to its source, the water is crystal clear and transparent.[6] Or take a bottle of wine or vinegar: the dregs are on the bottom, the heaviest, thickest particles, the lees, go to the bottom and at the top the liquid is clear and transparent. And for man it is the same thing: the dregs accumulate and settle below, and everything that is luminous and light rises to the brain or even higher, to the spirit.

Purity is on the heights and that is where we must go to find it. It cannot be found in the vegetative life, nor in the instinctive life, because they are too far down. And to find purity you must live the spiritual life. Then you will be free from intellectual error, free from the pain and longing of the heart, free from the dirt and illness of the physical body. Purity manifests itself in all of man's activities, in the food he eats, his gestures, his feelings and thoughts. But the source of purity is in spirituality and purity can only be attained by opening the doors of your soul to the spiritual life and letting in the rays of the sun: the love of God and His Wisdom.

You have no idea how I bathed in this morning's purity, how I plunged into the purity of the dawn! Usually there are battles going on in the atmosphere, it is not easy to find the right conditions for inner purification, but today, this morning... how could anyone not see the river flowing through the universe, in which you can bathe and purify yourself? These are methods of purification, to purify yourself with the four elements, earth, water, air, and fire, and specially, the sun's rays... you should start doing these exercises as soon as possible, for it is dangerous to hold on to one's impurities, they are the reason for all illness and disintegration.

Life itself is what brings purity. Let life circulate inside and purify you! As long as you are alive, the life that flows and circulates in you will throw off the poisonous and destructive elements, but when life slows down, then impurities install themselves, putrefaction sets in. That is why you must let life flow! Life renews itself like a spring, it rejects impurities. That is what it says in the Living Book of Nature.

'Not everyone is spiritual and yet they are alive, they get things done!' Yes, they may be alive, but only on the vegetable, animal, emotional, and possibly intellectual levels. On the higher level, in the glorious realm of the Spirit, they are dead. When one is dead on the higher plane, it is not long before one dies on the other planes. In Bulgaria, we say that a fish starts to become rotten in the head. The same is true for people who are ignorant of the truth and let their head rot, who abandon the spirit: the poison gradually spreads into the cells and throughout the entire system. When a man is dead spiritually, he is first of all a corpse on the higher planes, and then he dies in each one of the other planes: intellectually, he ceases to understand things, emotionally he is blasé and disgusted, sick at heart; in his instinctive life, he loses control more and more over his impulses; finally in his vegetable life, the roots decay and the tree begins to die. My dear brothers and sisters, when I talk about life, I do not mean vitality but spirituality, where life is most subtle and pure.

I ask you to retain this: when you introduce purity into your mind, you become luminous and intelligent; when you introduce purity into your heart, you become happy; when you introduce purity into your will, you become all-powerful; when you introduce purity into your blood, you become healthy. You see, it is mathematical, divine mathematics, divine algebra! On that level also there exist absolute equations.

Meditate on what I have said today, meditate on it all day, all your life long, nothing is more important. Put aside the rest, the needless, useless gossip and chatter. I have been waiting for twenty-nine years for you to understand that after a lecture such as this, you should leave the Hall in silence, reflecting upon the great mysteries of life you have just heard. But you rush to start chattering again, making as much racket as possible as if you were glad to get away from the misery of being silent and harmonious for a few hours, like school children tossing away their books when school is over... free at last! Hurrah for freedom!

This is where you hear the profound truths, dear brothers and sisters, truths that are essential for your future, but you cannot bear anything profound for very long. Listen to yourselves, you will hear the noise you make when I have left. And consequently, you make very little progress, everything you hear is immediately forgotten, erased, it has no chance to work on your brain. You must learn to let these great truths simmer inside you undisturbed so that they can have an effect.[7] When I talk to you, I put all my heart and soul and might into what I say, so that my words may have an effect on you... but you do not notice. The next day you come back and listen to yet another lecture: a whole life goes by that way.

How many times have I said to take one of the lectures, just one of the lectures, and make it the basis for your entire life. If you place the essential in the centre of your life, you will be surprised at how easily all the rest falls into place around this centre, the essential, the spiritual life. This does not mean that you reject all the rest... even the greatest Masters and Initiates for whom the only thing that counts is the spiritual life, look after their health, they take care of their bodies, eat, wash, dress, and work: on earth all that is indispensable. But actually, the material side of life is to them simply the means of attaining their goal. Their soul and spirit live entirely on the spiritual plane.

And now, dear brothers and sisters, I will tell you this: I, Omraam Mikhaël Aïvanhov, I know people here in this world who live the life of the spirit. They have been blackened and slandered and dragged through the sewer, but they remain steeped in the divine life which continually purifies and sanctifies them... to the discomfiture of the creatures of darkness. If you are a little puddle of water, a pond, you can be soiled very quickly, but if you are a whole ocean, who can soil you?

The Bonfin, 26th August, 1966

Notes

1. See *'Et il me montra un fleuve d'eau de la vie'*, Synopsis Coll., Part VII, chap. 1: 'Le talent ne suffit pas'.
2. See *'In Spirit and in Truth'*, Izvor Coll. n° 235, chap. 11: 'In Spirit and in Truth'.
3. See *The Philosopher's Stone – in the Gospels and in Alchemy*, Izvor Coll. n° 241, chap. 3: 'You are the salt of the earth'.
4. See *Truth: Fruit of Wisdom and Love*, Izvor Coll. n° 234, chap. 14: 'Scientific Truth and the Truth of Life'.
5. See *Le vrai travail de la mère pendant la gestation*, Brochure n° 318.
6. See *'Et il me montra un fleuve d'eau de la vie'*, Synopsis Coll., Part IX, chap. 1: 'Le fleuve de la vie divine'.
7. See *The Path of Silence*, Izvor Coll. n° 229, chap. 8: 'Silence, the Essential Condition for Thought'.

Chapter Four

PURITY IN THE THREE WORLDS

The last few days I have been speaking about purity, dear brothers and sisters, purity on the physical plane, on the astral plane and on the mental plane. But that is not all, there are still many more things to say about purity.

When it is a question of purity on the physical plane, for the body, clothing, material objects and so on, the French use the word meaning clean, cleanliness. But purity does not belong to the physical plane, it corresponds to the higher realm of the heart, of feelings and emotion. Purity and cleanliness are two different things; you can be clean without being pure, and pure without being clean. In India for instance, saddhus and yogis are tremendously pure in thought and feeling, but outwardly, my God! No one could say they are clean. In Europe, people wash themselves several times a day, but they are not pure inwardly. Like cats, there is no cleaner animal, he is always washing himself, but he is not pure. He is not pure because all he thinks about is catching a mouse and when he does he swallows it whole, without removing even the entrails. A lot of people are like cats... but you already know that.

If we go up a little higher and try to express purity on the mental plane, in the realm of thoughts, we find the words, saint, sainthood, saintliness. The Seraphim seen by St. John around the Throne of God, were not chanting, 'He is clean, the Lord is clean, He is clean...' Neither did they sing, 'He is pure, He is pure,' but *'Holy, Holy, Holy, Lord God Almighty...'* Thoughts belong in the realm of intention, of motive and goal. When, having reached a high stage of intelligence and being in possession of the light, your purpose is to accomplish God's will and carry out His plans, then you are holy, or sanctified.

The Hebraic language has different terms for purity for each one of the three planes, physical, astral and mental. The physical body is called *gouf,* the adjective for clean is *tsah*. The heart is called *nephesch*, and the adjective is *tam* or pure. The spirit is *rouah,* or for the divine soul, *neschama,* and the corresponding adjective is *kadosch,* holy, sanctified. The saints are called *kedoschim*. So you see *tsah, tam,* and *kadosch* all mean pure, but are applied to different elements. Actually for *nephesch*, there is a more appropriate adjective than *tam,* which is *tahor*. In the *Psalms* it says:

Lev Tahor bara li Elohim
(Lord, create in me a pure and contrite heart)
Ve rouah kadscheha al tiqar mi méni
(and take not from me Thy Holy Spirit)

Other languages undoubtedly have words that correspond.

Before, when you heard the word purity, you thought of it in a very general way, but now that we have discussed cleanliness, purity, saintliness, it will be easier for you to distinguish. In the *Lord's Prayer* it says, *'Our Father which art in Heaven, Hallowed be Thy Name,'*[1] hallowed meaning sacred, sanctified, holy, but not purified, nor cleansed, nor washed. Sanctification is a form of purification, but it is not the same purity as on the astral plane. Sanctification is linked to the world of thought, it is in the light of our highest thoughts that the name of God should be hallowed or sanctified.

The word saintliness implies light. In Bulgaria, as I have told you many times, we are more precise, we have words for each meaning: a saint is *svetia*, sainthood is *svetost*, the light is *svetlina*. Az *svetia* means I am filled with light, or shining; the world is *svet*. A saint, therefore, is one who has a light that makes him shine (the light that created the world) and that light is what makes him saintly. In French, the words saint, light, shine, world, have different roots; in Bulgarian, svetia, svetost, svetlina, az svetia, have the same root. Remarkable! Generally when we speak of a saint we refer to his quality of purity, never to his light... as though there was no light. Whereas actually saintliness is a quality of light, the pure light that shines on the mental plane along with intelligence and comprehension.

'Hallowed be Thy Name,' but where? In Church, in homes? No, in our heads, our thinking, that is where the Name of God should be sanctified. To sanctify the Name of God, you have to know Him, to understand Him in all His Glory. You say, 'All the world understands that.' No, if all the world understood the Name of God, things would be different. It is also said, *'The Eternal Life is to know Thee the only true God and Christ Jesus whom Thou hast sent.'* To sanctify the Name of God is to know His qualities, His properties, His virtues, in order to understand Him, and how He created the world. A tremendous, glorious work, that of knowing the Name of God and of sanctifying the Name of God!

One point I must explain: I told you that one could be clean without being pure and pure without being clean, which is true, but something needs to be added: it is impossible to become a saint before being entirely pure. To be saintly, one must first be pure.

In the past, people depended on gas lamps for light, each day the housewife had to remove the smoke from the glass. That is purity: a clean glass through which can shine the light of sainthood, we purify ourselves so that our inner light can shine through. Each one of us has a spark inside, but when the glass is dirty, it does not show through. That little image explains everything I am trying to say: when a man becomes pure, saintliness will manifest through him. Purity is the condition for the attainment of sainthood: when the soul manifests itself in his heart, a man is pure; when the spirit manifests itself in his mind, he is holy.

Holiness comes from above, from God; purity comes from below, from the physical plane where man sorts and selects and cleanses what he absorbs. If you pour pure water into an unwashed cup, what happens? God fills our cups (our brain, our heart, our whole being is a cup) but the cup must be cleansed. You say, 'I have been holding my cup up to God for a long time!' Maybe so, but God's answer is, 'As long as your cup is not clean, I will not pour anything into it.' Men hold up the oddest receptacles to be filled by God... excuse me for saying this, but sometimes they even hold up a chamberpot. And so the Heavenly Beings say to each other, 'If we fill this receptacle with ambrosia, it will do nothing but harm.' Sometimes the Heavenly Beings leave us empty for our own security.

This is a tremendously important subject, dear brothers and sisters, and you should reflect upon it. Holiness comes from God, but purity can only come from us, we are the ones to create it in us. Saintliness comes from above, before the Holy spirit visits us we cannot be saints. But when the Holy Spirit does come, it means that we are pure and by His Presence we are sanctified.[2]

The *Lord's Prayer* also says, *'Thy Will be done on earth-as it is in Heaven.'* You see, *'Thy Will'*. Why do the Initiates try so hard to accomplish God's Will? Because it is a magic act. In trying with all their might to do the Will of God, they link themselves to Him, and it is this union that makes them pure and sanctified. You say, 'But how? Purity has nothing to do with it!' Yes, it has. When someone wants to do the Will of God, his whole being is occupied, reserved, closed to other influences; the wills that are in opposition to God's Will, the other wills that want to use him, cannot. He is otherwise engaged, he keeps his purity. When man does not work to do the Will of God, that other will, visible or invisible, of the elementals, the larvae, even of other humans, tries to infiltrate inside him so as to use him, and all the opposing, discordant wills of his neighbour, his wife, his cousins and his aunts, etc., make him vulnerable and all the impurities pour into him. Yes, whoever does not want to do the Will of God is neither pure nor holy... a revelation for those of you who have not understood that!

You now know that you must work to accomplish God's Will, and save all your forces, your free time and your purity for that purpose, because if you are not occupied by God, you can be sure others will occupy you. You will have to serve and obey other wills, dangerous, selfish or anarchistic wills. As long as man does not understand that he must serve only God, then his hotel, his house or shop, that is, his entire being, will be unprotected, open to the wind, to tourists and undesirables of all kinds, and that is not the way to aquire purity.

You see, real purity, holiness, is not where people look for it. It comes from above. A river flows down from the mountain tops: if you drink its water at the source, the spring, it is pure, but lower down it becomes dirty, polluted, contaminated. You must go to the heights to find pure water, to the summit where God is. That water will not only cleanse you and quench your thirst, it will give you life, and that life will make you immortal. This is the true philosophy. Not everyone who preaches on the subject of holiness understands this magic fact. Below, you will not find holiness, but cleanliness, and even then more often than not what you find is not cleanliness but dirt.

Now, looking for symbols of purity in Nature, what do you find? On earth, purity is symbolized by precious stones, crystal, and above all, the diamond, the hardest of all stones. In the vegetable kingdom, the symbol of purity is the lotus, born in water, whose petals are extraordinarily limpid. You say, 'What about the lily? And the rose?' Yes, the lily is pure, but the rose is more a symbol of divine love. Among birds, the dove is the symbol of purity, which is why the Holy Spirit is always shown in the form of a dove. There is also the gentle lamb with its white fleece, innocence and humility. In the astral world, the angels, 'devas' as they are called, are the symbol of purity. Going higher up, there are other symbols of purity in the different kingdoms, all the way to God, absolute Purity, absolute Holiness. Think about this, meditate on the extraordinary fact that a disciple should want one thing only, to do God's Will, in order to protect, purify and sanctify himself. If not, whether he wants it or not, he will be constrained to obey other wills that will not be disinterested, selfless, pure or luminous. One should never force oneself to obey human wills as many people do, no matter how dishonest or criminal. When human wills, projects and tendencies correspond with God's Will, that is, if they want only the best for mankind and work only for the happiness, plenitude, health, beauty and freedom of the whole world, then obey them! But if the goal is personal and petty, do not obey.

I will give you an example to show you that humans do not know how to read in the Living Book of Nature. When you leave a few crumbs of food around, why is it that all kinds of insects immediately gather, ants and hornets, etc., to feast on them? Because dirt attracts them. Clean up the leavings, sweep them away, the insects disappear. In the same way, you should know that by harbouring impurities in your thoughts and feelings, you attract undesirables that like to feed on such things, and afterwards you can no longer get rid of them. Even if you kill the insects or chase them all away, as long as the dirt is there, more insects will always gather. The only way to get rid of them entirely is to remove the dirt, and then they will have to go elsewhere for their nourishment. On the astral plane, leftovers in the way of thoughts and feelings also ferment and rot and it is the same law, if we get rid of this impurity within ourselves, the undesirables will go.

As long as we do not entirely understand what purity is, that is, if we do not know what it is on every plane, we will never be pure. You say, 'But take little children, they may not understand, but they are pure.' God knows whether they are pure or not... and for how long! If a young girl is ignorant, she will lose her purity very quickly, because she is pure by chance, not deliberately, and in her ignorance, she will not know how to hold on to her purity. That is why young people must be taught what purity really is. You say, 'Yes, but it still is not clear, you haven't given us a real definition.' I will give you definitions, don't worry... at the moment, I am preparing the ground.

Suppose you find yourself with a group of people whose conversation and attitude are of a very coarse nature. When you return home, you have an impression of being soiled in some way, you feel the need to bathe in clear water. If you do, you free yourself of this uncomfortable impression and you feel light again. What is the conclusion? You should study your feelings and reactions. Sometimes you feel that you have been in the sewer, something slimy has rubbed off on you... you may be clean to all outward appearances, but inside, you are uncomfortable and feel the need to wash. Or sometimes without knowing why, you suddenly feel light and pure... do you ever analyse these different states of mind? Probably not, yet this is the way God teaches us, our feelings convey information and instructions that are precise and exact, and we should listen.

You say, 'But feelings are not always exact or objective, you can't trust feelings. The only things you can be sure of are things you can see and touch, weigh and measure, that remain the same and don't change, those things are sure and permanent. But emotions and the subjectivity of the psychic plane are not reliable.' Well, you are wrong, for there too the factors are determined, the measures absolute. Humans have rejected everything to do with the subjective world. The rapidity and subtlety of psychic phenomena have kept them from discovering or inventing instruments capable of grasping what goes on in the realm of feelings and thought, they have abandoned all this to the esoterists, to mediums, to Initiates. This is regrettable. When they finally have to investigate that realm, they will find the same mathematical precision and exactitude as on the physical plane.

Life is the essential. To put all your faith in what is dead, rigid, crystallised, with the pretext that it is easier to investigate those things and to set aside and abandon everything that is alive, is not very intelligent. Life obeys precise laws; to study it, you have only to know what aspect to dwell on. On the Rocher at sunrise, sometimes you have a calm, limpid, light feeling, yes, a wonderful, enchanting, ethereal feeling, and if you analyse this feeling you will see that it is actually more real than physical, material objects. When you feel that you have been in a sewer because of something you've read or a conversation you've exchanged with someone, a glance you have intercepted, analyse this feeling of impurity... you will see that there also exist absolute measures in the subjective, invisible world.

Now, you are going to say, 'But how do I know what is pure and what is impure?' It is very easy. Someone was telling me not long ago that there was no way of knowing what is good, what is bad, what is just and what is unjust, etc., I said to him, 'Really? You have no way of knowing? Well, look, when you have a desire to slap someone, hard... give yourself a slap before giving it to anyone else, and you will know at once that it is not the best thing! Something that is not good for you is not good for anyone else.' When we receive a slap, do we know that it is not a good thing? My God, how quickly we become intelligent.

When we are the ones to be affected, we always know what is good and what is bad. Wound someone, make someone angry, insult or rob someone, and you will see how well he knows the rules, including his legal rights! But when it comes to doing something to others, it is curious, he no longer knows right from wrong. It is easy to know, he has only to put himself in their place. Jesus summed up this great truth in the words, *'Whatsoever ye would that men should do to you, do ye even so to them...'* These words contain the essence of morality.[3]

But let us come back to purity. When the scribes and Pharisees brought the woman taken in adultery before Jesus, they wanted to stone her to death, as the law of Moses commanded. What did Jesus do? He traced on the ground (it has never been revealed that the signs were Kabalistic), and said, *'He that is without sin among you, let him first cast a stone at her!'* meaning that only those who were pure were entitled to criticize or state an opinion. As they all recalled having been dishonest in some way, they were afraid. They recognized the symbols traced by Jesus in the sand (indicating that punishment would be the reward of the impure) and one by one they disappeared, leaving the woman with Jesus. Jesus turned to her and asked, *'Where are thine accusers? Hath no man condemned thee?' 'No man, Lord.' 'Neither do I condemn thee... go, and sin no more.'* Everyone knows this story but not everyone understands it. You say, 'What do you mean, priests and ministers are always preaching about it!' Yes, that is the trouble, everyone preaches but no one understands.

Why can't we see that it is always the impure who accuse others of impurity? Why did Jesus, who was perfectly pure, not accuse the woman of impurity, or sin? My conclusion is that all who see impurity in others and condemn it relentlessly, are themselves impure; those who are really pure never criticize anyone who is not pure, even though they have earned that right because of their own purity. They are above all that. Jesus had the right to accuse the woman taken in adultery and did not, because the pure do not bother with the impurity of others.

Pure people try to purify other people and those who are impure try to soil and slander other people. It is not noble to throw dirt at others! Leave them to God's justice: if a man is not pure, Heaven will take away the beauty, the qualities, the ability, the blessings he has been given. It is not up to you to judge him. If you throw dirt on someone who lives a pure life, he will only become purer, no matter what you do he will be luminous and powerful and you will eat your heart out thinking, 'No matter what I do, I can't seem to hurt him.' Yes, that is the sad lot of all who think themselves pure and in a position to judge others. If someone is pure as a spring you cannot possibly dirty him, therefore instead of criticizing, why not emulate him and become a spring yourself, flowing and purifying itself ceaselessly?

For years I have known and understood too many more important things to bother with the impurity of others; on the contrary, I accept them as they are, I try to help them, I give them my love, my light, and if they do not understand, then too bad for them! If they do not choose this path, this light, sooner or later they will be in such a state of rot and decay that people will hold their noses and avoid them. Impure people are those who are always dissatisfied with life, and who, instead of working to realize a high ideal, do nothing but watch and spy on others, and then spread doubt and suspicion about them. That is impurity! To be full of suspicion, jealousy, envy, is to be truly negative.

Now, in order to complete what I said yesterday, I will draw your attention to something else you have not noticed which may be helpful to you. When you drink a cup of coffee or some other stimulant, as your forces begin to circulate inside you become more active, better disposed, your faith, hope and understanding increase: this stimulation of the nervous energies also affects the others realms. Other times, you are a bit anemic and apathetic, your vitality is down and all the rest along with it, your thoughts are not lucid, your willpower is weak, you have lost all self-confidence. On the outside nothing has changed, but inside there has been a general weakening of your entire being. When the vital force comes back in one way or another, again there is hope, again you are busy making plans.

It is not surprising that young people and all those who have great vitality, have more hope, more courage, more joy, more love than those who are old and tired, who are the pessimists who walk along sadly with their heads hanging down. Jesus said, *'I am come that they might have abundant life,'*[4] because he knew how important a role life plays. Not of course, the purely biological life. All who have that life, that vital force, think they have no need for Jesus or anyone else to come and give it to them. But that is not the life that produces results on the spiritual plane. The vital forces in the stomach, the belly, the lungs, the sexual organs, urge man to think only of eating, drinking, fighting, sleeping with women, etc.

When Jesus talked of life, he was alluding to the spiritual life, because that is the real life, the only life that offers the opportunity to be fulfilled, to blossom out. As soon as we begin to live in the currents that come directly from God, we become noble, loyal, wise and strong, life urges us to project light, hope, and love everywhere we go. The spiritual life is able to awaken in man the best thoughts and feelings. It is because they have abandoned that life that humans are becoming more and more sensual, greedy, gross, cruel and base. Yes, the spiritual life, dear brothers and sisters, is worth thinking about: how to attain it, how to keep it flowing. It is not easy of course, it comes from very high up, you have to install a whole piping system inside to make it circulate and flow so that you can bathe in it and be inspired by it. As soon as you have the spiritual life, you see immediately what the advantages are.

If Jesus prayed for his disciples to have this life, it is because they did not yet have it. Of course, they had something that came close, but not the quintessence of the spiritual life, they did not possess that yet. And if Jesus told them he would send them the Spirit, it was because they had not yet received it. Christians think the apostles were ready to receive the greatest revelations... no, Jesus had to prepare them and make them ready, Jesus interceded for them so that they would receive the spiritual life, that is, eternal life.[5] Eternal life is not an infinity of time, but the spiritual, inner life. Eternity can be a single second. It is not the length of time that makes life eternal but the quality of the spiritual life, the divine life.

Even if humans are not meant to live eternally, they can live the eternal life; it has never signified an eternity of life on earth as was thought by members of the sect whose belief was immortality. If they died, to them it was accidental, never because of the will of God. Curious, isn't it? Many Christians are still under such illusions, and they are not the only ones, many sects hold on to erroneous concepts. But one day, all this will be revised. Some of you are thinking, 'But you too, your Teaching is a sect.' No, no, our Teaching is the only one that is not a sect. One day I went so far as to say that even the Catholic Church is a sect for the moment, because it does not accept certain universal truths. Yes, in spite of the fact that the word catholic means universal, the Catholic Church is sectarian. Our Teaching is the universal Teaching that will one day be accepted all over the world.

You say, 'Well, of course, you preach for your own chapel!' In the first place it is not a chapel, if it had been I would have abandoned it long ago... yes, I would have been the first to go. Do you know why we have no temple or chapel? Because a chapel made by human hands would always be too small and limited. There already is a temple, the temple of God, which is the whole universe, so it is not really necessary to build another one. Besides, we are ourselves a temple, a little temple in which we officiate at the Divine Service. Yes, inwardly, we should be in our proper temple as much as possible. A lot of people do not know how to pray to God unless they are in church, they think God is nowhere but in church! Those people must learn how to enter their own temple. It says in the Scriptures, *'Ye are the Temple of the living God.'*[6]

You are yourself a living temple, and you should keep this temple clean and pure. Christians let their temple get broken down and dirty, and then once a year they go to a temple built by human hands. Well, that is too little, they will never be transformed! Each day you must be in your own temple and never leave it except to go from time to time into the great temple of Nature. That is the philosophy of the future, the religion of the future. Then, yes, there will be hope for man that he will change and be transformed, because day and night he will be purifying his temple and caring for it so that God and all His Angels can come and install themselves. Instead of which he goes once a year and lights a candle! Ridiculous! Grotesque! Once a week is too little.

Before men were as evolved as they are now, they fixed a day of the week for Church: in the new religion it will be seven days a week! All week long, all your life long! One day is too easy... you spend six days a week lying and trafficking, committing adultery, and then on the seventh day you go to church for a few minutes, dip your hand in holy water, and there you are! If it were that easy, there would have been better results. I, in any case, do not believe in it, I am the worst infidel and skeptic in existence. I do believe, I am a believer, but I believe in things that are more efficacious. You say, 'What you say is dreadful!' No, the founders of religions were psychologists, great educationalists with a profound knowledge of human nature, they knew what they were doing, that the time must be right before you can ask too much of human beings, and for the time being the instructions and regulations were necessarily limited.

But now the time is coming when everyone will say, 'What, only one day a week for church? No, I want to go to church all day long, all night, I want to sleep every night in church!' What church? Their own inner church, their temple, because if you start carrying your mattress into a church, you will see what will happen! And so, with the new religion, people will eat, drink, sleep, talk and embrace each other in their own church, in keeping with sacred rules. You say, 'My God, what an upheaval!' Yes, but a happy one. Rules are made for a certain epoch, and now the rules will be changed, there will be a new philosophy, a new religion, the religion of the living Christ: the Solar Religion. It has been deformed for centuries, but now people will know the truth at last.

My dear brothers and sisters, why bother to seek anything more than the spiritual life, because when the spiritual life comes, it will turn on your inner instruments and your brain will begin to think better, your heart will rejoice better, your willpower will surmount obstacles better, your physical body will be healthier and more vigourous, and you will do your work better.

As I was saying a while back, when someone loses his vital force, he can't see or feel anymore, as if he were already dead; his organs, his faculties are still there, nothing has been removed, it is only his vital force that is missing. Now, suppose the vital force comes back: everything starts to work again. It is the same with the spiritual force: man has centres, chakras and energies for the most part unknown;[7] if they do not function it is because there is no current, no petrol, no spiritual energy to set them going. The day this energy manifests itself, it will awaken all the centres, not only physical ones, but psychic, spiritual centres, and man will perceive that other creatures, other powers, other forces exist and circulate. A whole wealth of discoveries will open up for him all the way to infinity, because of the work, the research, he has done over the years.

The flowers you have picked start to fade: put them in water, they come to life again. A carrot that is wilted is dipped in water and in no time is as good as new. What happens? God has put a whole science in these minor phenomena that occur around us, but you pay no attention, you do not notice that everything is connected, and that is why the meaning of life eludes you.

You are wondering how little things can be so revealing to me? Because I study the Living Book of Nature one letter at a time, word by word, and I discover extraordinary things.

When I speak of the new life, dear brothers and sisters, I mean the same spiritual life that Jesus talked about. Only with that life will there be purity. That is why the Initiates always try to come close to the divine Spring, to become part of the Spring themselves, to obtain purity and taste it all the time as a feeling of lightness, of limpidity and freshness, for that is the property, the feeling of the spiritual life. The spiritual life is what makes you feel clean, washed and purified... sanctified... night and day.

Know this: purity is not where people look for it. Only in the divine life can purity be found, and I repeat, when you live the divine life, no one can make you dirty, even if they cover you with smut and slander, no one can tarnish or corrupt you. But without the divine life, no matter what you do you will still feel impure, something foul and sticky attaches itself to you that you cannot get rid of. Sometimes people are convinced of their own guilt and keep repeating, 'I am damned, I am damned...' when they have actually committed no crime, they simply feel impure: the divine life has never visited them.

But once the divine life comes to stay, nothing and no one can make you dirty because dirt does not come from the outside... dirt comes from inside. Jesus said, *'There is nothing from without a man that entering into him can defile him: but the things which come out of him, those are they that defile the man...'* [8]

You see, it is written.

The Bonfin, 28th August, 1966

Notes

1. See *'Notre Père'*, Brochure n° 313.
2. See *The Mysteries of Fire and Water,* Izvor Coll. n° 232, chap. 18: 'The Coming of the Holy Spirit'.
3. See *'Cherchez le Royaume de Dieu et sa Justice'*, Synopsis Coll., Part V: 'Tu aimeras ton prochain comme toi-même'.
4. See *Sons and Daughters of God,* Izvor Coll. n° 240, chap. 1: 'I came that they may have life'.
5. See *'You Are Gods'*, Synopsis Coll., Part VIII: 'Living in eternal life'.
6. See *'Cherchez le Royaume de Dieu et sa Justice'*, Synopsis Coll., Part III: 'Vous êtes le temple du Dieu vivant'.
7. See *Man's Subtle Bodies and Centres – the Aura, the Solar Plexus, the Chakras...*, Izvor Coll. n° 219, chap. 6: 'The Chakras'.
8. See *The Philosopher's Stone – in the Gospels and in Alchemy,* Izvor Coll. n° 241, chap. 2: 'It is not what goes into the mouth that defiles a person'.

Chapter Five

THE RIVER OF LIFE

We have seen in earlier lectures on the subject of the ten Sephiroth (*Kether, Chokmah, Binah, Chesed, Geburah, Netzach, Hod, Yesod,* and *Malkuth*),[1] that the ninth Sephira, *Yesod,* which means foundation, presides over purity. Now we will see why *Yesod* is considered to be the foundation, the base.

The Lord *Shaddai El Hai,* whose name means literally Almighty Living God, reigns over the Sephira *Yesod.* He is also the distributor of life. The order of *Kerubim* (angels in the Christian religion) live in this Sephira under the leadership of the Archangel Gabriel, who presides at births. It is not by chance that the Gospels name Gabriel as the Archangel who appeared before Mary to announce the birth of Jesus, and to Zachariah, the husband of Elizabeth, to announce the birth of John the Baptist. The Moon (called *Levana* in the Hebraic) is the material aspect of *Yesod* and symbolic of the woman, and also of imagination, that is, any matter that can be shaped into different forms. It is also the symbol of purity. When a soul reincarnates, it must pass through the regions of the Moon on its way to earth to be born, and again on its way back to the other regions when it dies. The Moon thus presides at births and deaths, which shows you how involved it is with all the basic, fundamental issues in life.

People allude to the Moon in all kinds of ways, mostly derogatory: the Moon makes one moonstruck, moonfaced, moony; moonshine has a lunar (lunatic) effect and it appears that moonstroke is worse than sunstroke... but those are things having to do with the lower aspect of the Moon. There are several other aspects, but to make things easier, we will say two aspects: one, the twilight region of illusion, deception, madness and aberration, and the other, a region of absolute purity, of absolute clarity of vision. Poets prefer the twilight region, they like fantasy, imagination, the unreal, but all this vagueness and lack of precision is not without danger... many poets have ended their days in madness.

Each Sephira represents a world and each world has its own hierarchy. The lower region of *Yesod* is cloudy and dustfilled, that is, full of illusion, deviation, wildness. Yes, *Yesod* is where the psychic life begins, and that life is composed of vague, shadowy forms. Those who have not gone further and developed knowledge through study and meditation, are victims of these illusive forms. *Yesod* is, of course, a much more subtle region than *Malkuth,* the side of the Moon which is near *Malkuth* is still foggy, damp and full of dust. But it is a region that must be traversed if you wish to reach the world of light in *Tiphareth,* the Kingdom of the Sun.

Now let us see why *Yesod* is the Sephira of purity. We have seen that *Shaddai El Hai* is the distributor of life, and that the *Kerubim.* (or angels) receive this life and transmit it to humans. We have seen that life is a current, a river that comes from the heights, from the Spring: the River of Life is the Christ. That is why Jesus said, *'I am the way, the truth and the life.'*[2] An Initiate hearing those words has before him a mental image of a river coursing down the mountainside and melting into the sea. The way, the truth and the life, what do those words signify? The way is the riverbed, life is the water that flows along the riverbed, the truth is the Spring, the beginning of everything, from which life and all creatures come. Another interpretation: the riverbed meandering along is wisdom winding its way back up to the Spring, Truth, whilst the water is love, or life (life must be love since it is born of love). Jesus meant, I am the way of wisdom; I am the water of love transporting the divine life; I am the fountain, the high source of truth from which flow the waters of life to refresh all creatures. Water is the symbol of love: the energies and forces circulating in Nature and the Cosmos are the fluid, the water, that quenches thirst and restores life. An exercise that should be done every day is to imagine that you go to the spring to drink at the source of the river and refresh yourself with the purest and most limpid water, remaining close to it as long as possible. The effects of this exercise are incalculable. The spring and the river in the image are related, as you see, to the spiritual life, to this Teaching which is based on love, or water; wisdom, or the riverbed, and Truth, or the Spring.

Water flows down the mountainside... one might say that it is thanks to the mountains that life exists on earth! The mountain-peaks are tall antennae through which the earth communicates with the sky, they form a link between Heaven and earth and capture heavenly forces and energies in the form of whirlwinds and luminous waves. Water that comes down from the mountaintops is in that way impregnated with celestial fluids.[3] Spirits that are disincarnated come and bathe in these fluids in order to reinforce themselves before carrying on their work of transforming the world.

Let us go on with this image of the river and see how much more there is to discover. The river starts high up on the mountaintop and flows down onto the plains. At its source, the water is still pure and crystalline but it has to go through regions where unscrupulous inhabitants throw peelings and other filth into the river without a thought for the inhabitants further down who will have to drink polluted water. Those who live further down do the same, and by the time the water reaches the plains, it contains enough poison to kill anyone who drinks it.

The river is a most meaningful and profound symbol. In the *Apocalypse,* the *Book of Revelation,*[4] the River of Life that refreshes all living creatures passes through the angelic Hierarchies, *the Seraphim, Cherubim, Thrones, Dominations, Powers, Virtues, Principalities, Archangels* and *Angels,* each one adding its own virtues and properties to the River. Finally the River comes to the region of the glorious souls where it refreshes and vivifies the Prophets, great Masters and Initiates, the Saints and all who are pure. But by the time the River comes to the region of average men, it is the same as in the plains: the water is polluted, people have dumped their garbage in it.

Humans unconsciously throw their worst thoughts and feelings into the River of Life and are compelled to swallow each other's refuse like toads and larvae in a swamp, they are too far from the pure water and have no choice. The swamp is an image of the world... yes, the world is a swamp into which 'frogs' and 'toads' and 'larvae' pour the refuse of their anger, their cruelty, their rancour, which everyone else will have to consume.

Like water, life takes on the colour, pure or impure, of the regions through which it circulates. Life has varying degrees and, depending on the regions it must traverse and the inhabitants of those regions, it either will or will not have certain properties. Everyone does not receive the same quality of life from the River. People say to me, 'That's life, Master, that's life!' And I answer, yes, but which life? The life of a toad? The life of a wild animal, a crocodile, or the life of an angel? The life God gave us has many different degrees. There is a form of life even in the subterranean regions, that nourishes the lowest creatures, for life must also feed and nourish the devils, otherwise how would they obtain life? Another god would have to exist, an adversary of God as mighty as He or even more so, to create life for them. No, no, the same God feeds us all, including the devils and demons. The difference is that they do not receive the purest food, they must be content with leftovers, scraps of food that are spoilt and tainted. That is the destiny of subterranean creatures: to have to be content with leftovers from the divine life.

A look at beggars will explain what I have just said: perhaps they are there to teach us a lesson, they say to us, 'Look at our lot, we didn't want to learn, we didn't want to work, and now we are reduced to looking in garbage cans for crusts thrown out by those more fortunate than we. We are like subterranean creatures who must content themselves with leftovers from the celestial life.' Beggars and tramps can teach the world a valuable lesson, but no one understands their language.

You ask, 'Are you saying that God feeds the inhabitants of Hell?' I know this idea will shock some of you, but think about it: these inferior beings, these tormentors of humanity, who gave them life if not God? God alone creates life; any other creator of life would have to be as omnipotent as God. As a matter of fact, that is something that has been a stumbling block to the Christian religion, the idea that God has someone who stands up to Him, an adversary He cannot overcome without human help! How could anyone accept such a thing? God alone holds life in His power and, in His generosity He keeps even the most inferior creatures from dying out completely, because they are all in His service.

When someone deserves a good lesson, it is not God (as people think) who stoops to give it to him. He says to those of His administrators who mete out justice (the devils), 'Go and find so and so and shake him up a bit to make him think!' If God considers these people useful to His work, He must give them sustenance... perhaps not the choicest parts nor the biggest, but at any rate He will feed them. That is how I explain God's generosity. There is always hope for evil creatures, if they repent and become pure, they will be able to return to God. This is true whether you believe it or not. Humans are so cruel they want to prevent devils from learning how to improve, they would prefer them to burn in Hell forever... whilst God prefers to wait for them to transform themselves, become good, and return to Him. He has infinite patience, He is not in a hurry, and that is why there are still devils to torment humans! It seems however that in a future epoch, the devils will no longer be able to torment people because they will be bound hand and foot. This epoch is now approaching.

I have already explained the significance of the Apocalyptic dragon.[5] In the Book of Revelation it says that the dragon will be bound and thrown into the abyss for a thousand years. And what then? Well, he will be educated and trained and when he emerges, he will no longer need fangs or claws or venom. Yes, he will go through intensive treatment in the workshops below and be given a good scouring. Don't think it is enough to shut a dragon up for a thousand years for him to come out transformed! A dragon cannot transform himself that easily, he has to be mistreated and handled a bit roughly before he will accept to change. There are people who will take care of this, they will see to it and tell him, 'See here: now it is your turn. Humans have been tormented by you long enough, now you are going to have to learn to be kind.'

How do I know these things? I read them. Where do I read them? In any case not in books written by humans, I am disillusioned with them because of all the errors and incoherence, I no longer waste my time on them. I read in the Living Book of Nature, which is where I discovered that the love of God, the life of God, reaches down even into the depths, the abysmal space. Even there a few particles of life exist, otherwise how would they survive? You say, 'But man creates life!' No, dear brothers and sisters, man does not create life, life comes from God, man simply transmits it, he cannot create life. If he could, he would be able to keep himself from dying. Man simply transmits life for a certain length of time, he is not its creator.

To get back to the image I gave you of the River of Life, of divine Life flowing down from the heights above into the depths of the earth: once there, it is purified of all the debris it has accumulated along the way in the factories at the earth's centre, where things are transformed with the help of all kinds of filters and screeners and sifters. Life receives a new form and then returns to the heights, which is exactly what the river does when it flows down the mountainside to the sea: the sun's rays turn its muddy and troubled waters into vapour, so that it can rise again and come back down in a new form, rain, or snow, or dew. The same phenomenon exists for the blood: it is pure when it starts down from the lungs, but then it passes through the heart and on down into the organs where it accumulates waste matter and has to go back up to the lungs to be purified. The circulation of the bloodstream, the circulation of water in the earth's riverbeds, are things I read in the Living Book of Nature where those things are inscribed, but humans have not noticed. God has inscribed His laws everywhere in Nature, God expresses Himself in the phenomena of Nature, but we prefer books written by sick people with distorted minds.

I will take the beggars, the tramps we were talking about a little while ago to show you how the external life corresponds with the inner life. People who can afford to dine in the best restaurants are served the best food, the finest quality; less affluent people have to be content with more modest restaurants and arc served stew, or soup... leftovers from the grander restaurants. Others, the beggars and tramps, have no possibility of going to a restaurant and search for crusts and leavings in the garbage cans. The wealthy eat the finest food, the poor must eat what others reject. In the psychic, spiritual world it is the same, only on that plane perhaps it is the rich who search for scraps in the garbage!

The same hierarchy exists in the inner life as in the outer life. Someone whose soul is filled with beautiful thoughts and feelings is nourished by celestial food. Someone who has gone too low down, who is caught in the lower grades of life because he thinks only in terms of his greed, grudges and gross needs, gradually becomes more and more impoverished, too poor to eat in the best restaurants of the spiritual world. Like a beggar, he has to eat what others reject, he has trouble forming his spiritual body because he has nothing pure or luminous to do it with... what he consumes is dark and dirty. The best way to escape having to absorb other people's leavings is to remain on the higher planes. The secret of the spiritual life is to climb as high as you can and stay there. You know that you must climb to the top of the mountains to find pure water to drink and to find the crystal clear water of divine Love you must climb all the way to the Spring. And you cannot eat and drink in the heavenly restaurants unless you are rich in virtues. `

Now let us study life and purity to see where the connection might be. We know that *Shaddai El Hai* is the Lord of Life who reigns over *Yesod,* the next to last Sephira on the Tree of Life. The image of a vertical tree adopted by the Kabala to describe the Sephiroth, does not imply that one Sephira is in any way superior to another. Each one of the ten Sephiroth, *Kether, Chokmah, Binah, Chesed, Geburah, Tiphareth, Netzach, Hod, Yesod,* and *Malkuth,* is a manifestation of a particular quality or virtue of God. There are not ten gods, but one God. *Shaddai El Hai* is the same as and equal to *Ehieh, El,* and *Elohim Gibor,* and appears in *Yesod* under the aspect of Creator and Distributor of life. There are no superior or inferior manifestations of God on the Tree of Life, the difference lies in the material the regions are made of: from *Kether* to *Malkuth,* the material grows progressively denser. There are no different degrees in the quality of God's attributes.

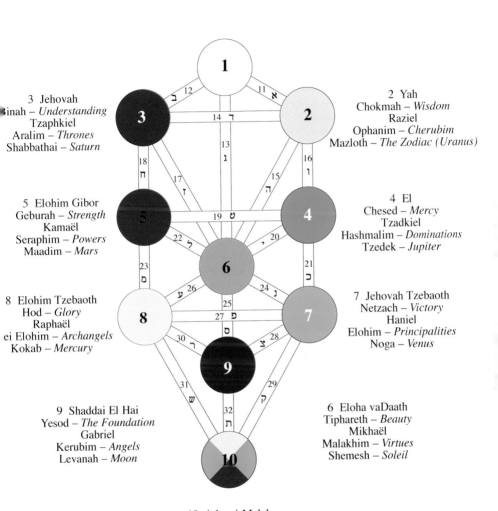

1 Ehieh
Kether – *The Crown*
Metatron
Hayot haKadesh – *Seraphim*
Rashith haGalgalim – *First Swirlings (Neptune)*

3 Jehovah
Binah – *Understanding*
Tzaphkiel
Aralim – *Thrones*
Shabbathai – *Saturn*

2 Yah
Chokmah – *Wisdom*
Raziel
Ophanim – *Cherubim*
Mazloth – *The Zodiac (Uranus)*

5 Elohim Gibor
Geburah – *Strength*
Kamaël
Seraphim – *Powers*
Maadim – *Mars*

4 El
Chesed – *Mercy*
Tzadkiel
Hashmalim – *Dominations*
Tzedek – *Jupiter*

8 Elohim Tzebaoth
Hod – *Glory*
Raphaël
Benei Elohim – *Archangels*
Kokab – *Mercury*

7 Jehovah Tzebaoth
Netzach – *Victory*
Haniel
Elohim – *Principalities*
Noga – *Venus*

9 Shaddai El Hai
Yesod – *The Foundation*
Gabriel
Kerubim – *Angels*
Levanah – *Moon*

6 Eloha vaDaath
Tiphareth – *Beauty*
Mikhaël
Malakhim – *Virtues*
Shemesh – *Soleil*

10 Adonai-Melek
Malkuth – *The Kingdom*
Sandalfon (Uriel)
Ishim – *Beatified Souls*
Olem HaYesodoth – *Earth*

Sephirotic Tree

It is not the ordinary life that *Shaddai El Hai* manifests as Creator and Distributor of Life, but the Life that comes from above, from the Spring that cleanses and purifies everything it touches and rejects all the impurities that would prevent its manifestation. In that way, purity is closely linked to life, the divine Life that purifies.

The Caduceus of Hermes has always been the symbol of power, the powers sought after by the Initiates such as the Magic Mirror, the Universal Panacea, the Elixir of Eternal Life, the Philosopher's Stone (and more, but those are the most important), each one corresponding to a Sephira on the Middle Pillar of the Tree of Life. The Caduceus of Hermes corresponds to *Kether*, the Magic Mirror to *Daath**, the Universal Panacea to *Tiphareth,* the Elixir of Eternal Life to *Yesod*... and the Philosopher's Stone to *Malkuth.*[6] As you see, the Elixir of Eternal Life corresponds to *Yesod* because *Yesod* represents purity, and the result of a life of purity is immortality.

You cannot be pure once you are dead, for where there is stagnation, there is fermentation, mildew, disintegration. After a long walk or after working for a long time, you are tired, you have to rest in order to allow the life in your bloodstream to get rid of the waste matter that has accumulated in your muscles. Work is a form of combustion, and like all combustion, it produces waste matter which must be removed, otherwise paralysis sets in, the muscles become paralysed. Life gets rid of this waste matter by directing it into other parts of the body to be expelled through the pores, the nose, the mouth, or other eliminatory organs, whereupon you revive, your strength comes back, you are ready to resume your exertions.

Every impurity, as I have said, is alien to the organism, and what is not part of the organism must be rejected. If life did not do this automatically, you would fall ill, first with fatigue, then with some illness that grows more and more serious until

* Daath signifies knowledge, learning. It is the 11th Sephira, rarely mentioned in the Kabala.

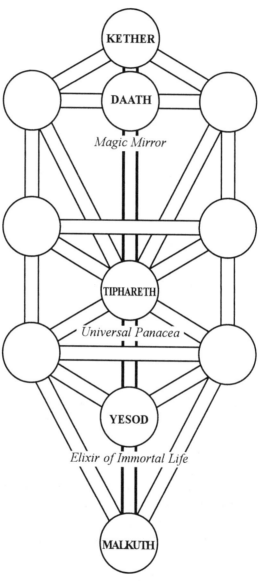

Caduceus of Hermes

KETHER

DAATH

Magic Mirror

TIPHARETH

Universal Panacea

YESOD

Elixir of Immortal Life

MALKUTH

Philosopher's Stone

The Central Pillar

you die. Fatigue is always a sign of waste matter accumulated in the nervous system, the lungs, liver, or muscles, and every opportunity must be given to the system to help it eliminate this accumulation.

Impurity, the cause of fatigue, even paralysis in extreme cases, is the enemy of life. Purity is life's friend, filling it with strength, health, and energy. You must seek purity on the three planes, cleanliness for the physical plane, purity for the astral plane, and saintliness for the mental plane. You know that on the physical plane if you eat food that is spoiled you fall ill, whereas if you follow a good nutritive diet, you are well-disposed, energetic, never tired. In a spiritual school, disciples not only nourish themselves well, but are careful to consume only the lightest food that will produce the least possible amount of waste matter, to abstain from eating meat or alcohol, which entail a large amount of waste matter that the system has trouble eliminating.

The same thing on the astral plane: when someone is sensual, over-loaded with waste matter psychically, the psychic system needs time to get rid of it. Those who allow themselves only subtle, luminous, ethereal and divine sensations, do not strain their nervous system and consequently need little time and little sleep to recover their vitality.

Do you see the advantages of living a pure life on every level? Not only will your health improve but your heart will rejoice, your mind will be clearer, enabling you to penetrate into the profound mysteries of Creation and conceive ideas of great significance for mankind. Otherwise, there will always be a veil, a screen that will prevent you from seeing and understanding the important things. Most humans lead an impure life. It is the greatest obstacle to understanding, learning and progress. This is the truth... you are free of course, not to believe it, but others before me have verified these truths, they have been valid since the beginning of time and will be throughout all Eternity.

Now here are a few methods for purification. There are external methods such as concentrating on a silver object (silver is related to the Moon), or bathing in water, but they only contribute to purification, they do not purify the whole being. If purity were a simple matter of holding a piece of silver in one's hand or of bathing in water, there would be nothing but angels on earth... which is not the case! Remember what I said in the last lecture: to purify yourself you must not only be cleansed but your thoughts and feelings must be lifted to a higher plane, you must entertain only thoughts and feelings that are pure, that is, unselfish and impersonal.

Water teaches us the two processes of purification: infiltration and evaporation. Through infiltration, water penetrates into the earth, deposits the dregs it has accumulated, and emerges purified and fit to drink. Symbolically it is the same for human beings, they are mistreated and crushed by other human beings or by events, until because of the suffering and sorrow and pressure they experience, they emerge purified.

Disciples choose another method: the sun purifies them, not the earth. As water evaporates under the effect of the sun's rays, the disciple who exposes himself to the rays of the spiritual sun is warmed and lifts himself upward, speaking symbolically. He is purified by the elements he absorbs from the etheric layers of the atmosphere, and then returns to earth to water the plants, the animals, and other humans. A disciple who works at purifying himself with wisdom and light is not submitted to suffering and sorrow.

The first method takes you down into the darkest depths of the earth, the second method teaches you to see, to contemplate and know all things by the light of the sun's rays. The water on the summits is more substantial and nourishing than the water that flows out of the earth's springs. Alchemists in the past always used rainwater or dew for their experiments because they contain heavenly forces, whereas spring water, even filtered, contains particles of crude matter. Water that is full of minerals does not clean as rainwater does.

There are a number of exercises for purification, but today I will give you the following easy ones. One thing I must tell you: it takes years of practice to obtain results.

Exercises

1. Imagine that you climb up thousands of meters to where you can grasp the Prana, or pure life. You let it pour down on you like celestial rain and penetrate deep into your cells. Keep imagining this until you feel lighter, better able to breathe, more clearsighted.

2. Go to the sunrise in the morning, look up at the sun, and imagine that you penetrate all the way to its centre and purify yourself in the sunlight.

3. Lie naked in the sun imagining that a breeze is passing through your entire body, carrying off all the impurities.

4. Do the same thing in water, a bath or the sea, being careful to choose a secluded place.

5. This exercise is with the earth: you go into the forest, stretch out, dig a little hole with your finger, and address the earth, 'O earth, you who have given me all the elements with which to form my body, I thank you. But I have a request: I ask you to take all my impurities down into your laboratories and in their place give me the purest materials so that I can accomplish my work in the world.' That is the way you speak to the earth. Then you pronounce the formula: Taro Tora Rota Tarota Rotaro. These are Kabalistic words of the utmost efficacity. Pronounce the formula and meditate for a few moments. The earth which is intelligent will hear you,

she will summon her workers to rid you of your impurities, and you will be free.

These methods are for you, dear brothers and sisters, but will you know how to appreciate them, will you practise them? By accepting the ideas I bring you, just by accepting them, you are sanctifying yourselves... yes, these ideas are sufficient to sanctify you. There are many more revelations to make to you, but the time is not right, you would not be able to bear them. Many things remain to tell you but you must be prepared for them.

The Bonfin, 28th August, 1966

Notes

1. See *Angels and other Mysteries of The Tree of Life,* Izvor Coll. n° 236, chap. 2: 'Introduction to the Sephirotic Tree of Life'.
2. See *'Et il me montra un fleuve d'eau de la vie,* Synopsis Coll., Part VII, chap. 5: 'Je suis le chemin, la vérité et la vie'.
3. See *The Mysteries of Fire and Water,* Izvor Coll. n° 232, chap. 7: 'Water is Born of Mountains'.
4. See *'Et il me montra un fleuve d'eau de la vie',* Synopsis Coll., Part XII, chap. 3: 'Et sur les deux bords du fleuve il y avait un arbre de vie'.
5. See *The Book of Revelations: A Commentary,* Izvor Coll. n° 230, chap. 10: 'The Woman and the Dragon', chap. 11: 'The Archangel Mikhaël Casts Out the Dragon', chap. 12: 'The Dragon Spews Water at the Woman', chap. 15: 'The Dragon is Bound for a Thousand Years'.
6. See *'Et il me montra un fleuve d'eau de la vie',* Synopsis Coll., Part V, chap. 2: 'Les séphiroth du pilier central. La séphira Daath'.

Chapter Six

PURITY AND PEACE

For the last few days, dear brothers and sisters, we have been discussing nothing but purity. Still, I think a few more words are needed to make this subject absolutely clear.

You have seen that it is not possible to be completely healthy, sound and happy without being pure, nor is it possible to be at peace. The Initiates know that the slightest impurity in their physical body robs them of peace in their thoughts and feelings, and that is why they attach so much importance to purity.

Peace comes as a result of harmony between all the elements in the human system, in the spirit, soul, mind, heart, will and in the physical body. The fact that it is so difficult to obtain proves how seldom the elements are in harmony. Even when a human being is intelligent enough to control his thinking, still in his heart there may be a base emotion that leads him into error and all kinds of indulgence. Or, although he may be inspired by lofty thoughts and feelings, his willpower may be too weak to function. How can there be peace in the midst of such confusion? Peace is man's ultimate attainment. Only after repeated failures alternating with victories, only after finally deciding to help his divine nature to triumph over the noisy and rebellious lower nature, will he know peace.[1] Before that, he may have a few peaceful moments, but nothing permanent.

That is why you hear so many people say, 'I can't find peace, peace does not exist as far as I am concerned.'

True peace once found is impossible to lose. There may be occasional agitations, but these are superficial, deep down inside there is peace. Once man achieves real peace inside himself, none of the upheavals that occur on the surface of the world can penetrate or disturb the state of peace he is in. He is protected, as in a fortress, the refuge of the higher Self. Psalm 91 says, ... *'He is my refuge and my fortress, My God, in Him will I trust...* '[2] Once man attains that high point of his being and holds fast, he knows peace, divine peace... but before reaching that peace, how many victories must be obtained over his baser thoughts, desires, and actions!

I can hear you saying to yourselves, 'What is he talking about? He said he was going to tell us more about purity!' Peace comes as a result of harmony between all the elements that constitute the human being, and harmony can exist only when the elements are pure; if they are not in harmony it means that impurities have somehow forced their way in. When you eat something that upsets you, it makes you irritable and ill, but as soon as you get rid of whatever it was, you recover: impurity destroys peace. To obtain peace therefore, the first thing to do is to purify yourself, eliminate all the material inside that might prevent your mind and heart and will from working together harmoniously. A true Initiate understands that the essential thing is to become pure, pure as crystal, pure as the light of the sun... because with this purity, he will be able to obtain all the rest. Naturally, it is not easy to obtain absolute purity: it must be understood first of all, then it must be loved and desired with every fibre of one's being, and lastly it must be realized on the physical plane.

If confusion and disorder reign in your physical body, in your heart and mind, it is because you have absorbed elements that are impure: an impurity is anything that is foreign to the system, any undesirable, alien matter which may not be impure of itself, but is nevertheless impure from the point of view of the structure of the physical or psychic system. When you are upset, it is because you have allowed some kind of impurity to enter in the guise of a thought, a feeling, or an action. Those impurities must be got rid of.

Some people complain that they seem to attract nothing but misfortune, 'Everything bad happens to me,' they say. 'I don't see why.' It is quite simple. You know what a lightning rod is, a conduit that draws the lightning to a particular place so that other places may be safe. Impurity is a form of lightning rod. Matter has the property of attracting similar matter, lightning attracts lightning, if you will. Each impurity that is deposited in your psychic, astral or mental bodies, will perforce attract a matching impurity in the form of waves and vibrations that correspond to it. The presence of impurities somewhere guarantees that lightning will hit that particular place sooner or later in the form of illness or trouble.

Today I give you a key: impurity on any plane, mental, astral or physical, means trouble. When I say trouble, it is the very least that can happen, for impurity can be fatal. It is essential to do everything you can to purify yourself on all levels: baths and purges, internal and external washings, and... prayer and meditation. Only then will you be safe.

All illness, physical or nervous, comes as a result of the presence, the invasion of impurities. Unfortunately, not realizing that we need to purify ourselves, we turn to external remedies, medicine of all kinds, but never to inward purification. You are thinking, 'People fall ill even when they are pure!' Obviously that is true, for the food and drink we consume, the air we breathe, are full of impurities we can do nothing about. As long as the earth is not pure, humans will go on being contaminated by the collective impurity. The human system is unable to reject all impurity; the foreign matter accumulates and eventually impedes the circulation of the blood, and the body develops arteriosclerosis, for instance. Nature originally meant for man to live for centuries, but because of the impurities he is obliged to take into his system, his destiny is now to deteriorate and die at a comparatively young age.

Of course, if we could swallow a mouthful of the Elixir of Eternal Life from time to time, every impurity would disappear... all the veins, arteries, and other channels would be open and clear and we would be young again! The Elixir of Eternal Life is no more than a liquid of utmost purity that clears the pipeline system of the physical body. It existed in ancient times and perhaps still does in some people, for actually this Elixir is spread about everywhere in Nature: in the earth, in oceans, in rivers, in mountains, in the atmosphere, in plants, and especially in the sun's rays, but in such minute doses that it would require a very special instrument to extract it and condense it. It is this Elixir that we try to seize as we watch the sunrise in the morning, the Elixir that circulates about in Nature like living water. Each minute little atom suspended in air is filled with this spiritual essence[3] and by concentrating on the sun, we fill our bodies with these particles that purify us, strengthen and invigorate us, and fill us with new life.

As he purifies himself, man introduces new life in himself. Even if he nourishes himself with only the purest thoughts and feelings, he will not rid himself at once of all the impurities he has accumulated in his other incarnations. But he will, if he goes on gradually increasing his purity during several reincarnations. As mankind evolves, so the world also evolves and transforms itself, and one day (in the distant future of course), all the rocks and stones, trees and plants and mountains, even human beings and everything that exists will be pure, luminous, transparent, radiant. It is part of God's plan.

Because I reveal to you that illness is the result of impurity, there is no reason to criticize everyone who happens to be ill, 'Ah, ah, he is ill because he is not pure, that is what the Master said.' No, people who lead a perfectly pure life may be overcome by impurities accumulated long ago in the past, and there is no need to reproach them now, all that is ancient history. I explain things to you as they are, but you have no right to use them against others.

Purity is what keeps us alive, and impurity is what makes us die: that is our destiny. We can do nothing about it except to try and improve the situation by becoming master of ourselves, gaining control by surveying our thoughts, our feelings, and our actions. More than that we cannot do, for the world is entirely contaminated. If we could eat and drink nothing but absolutely pure food, man would again live a long time, but where can we go to find food and drink that are pure? Where can we find air that is absolutely pure? The whole earth is poisoned. We can delay illness and death by harbouring nothing but the purest thoughts and feelings, but we cannot entirely eliminate them: the physical body depends for its health on the state of the world and the behaviour of human beings.

On the psychic plane it is possible to be nourished by pure, luminous and celestial food, but on the physical plane, man is obliged to absorb all kinds of impurities. The bread he eats is poisoned, the water he drinks is polluted. As for milk, they have tried all kinds of scientific methods to make it hygienic, cows are no longer milked by dirty hands, milking is done mechanically, the milk is controlled, sterilized, pasteurized, etc. Does this make it any better? Milk may not have germs in it, but neither does it contain any really nutritious elements! That is what needs to be studied and improved. When certain drawbacks are scientifically removed, others take their place! I don't mean that all scientific research is useless or harmful, no, on the contrary, it is thanks to research that human life is prolonged. We will look into this subject again at another time.

One day, the question of purity will be investigated in every domain and whether it is called hygiene or sanity or any other name is unimportant, we will always be seeking purity... in order to prolong life, in order to cure disease and illness, in order to fill the lives of human beings with joy and happiness.

My dear brothers and sisters, from now on think about purity, concentrate on purity night and day, it will have a wonderful effect on you... not to be pure for vanity's sake, but because you feel the need of purity for yourself and for the good of the whole world, so that everyone may benefit. To help others, you must first learn how to help yourself. Someone says, 'Let me remove the speck of dirt on your face!' and because his hands are dirty, he adds his dirt and your face is dirtier than before. To see someone else's impurities is easier than to see your own, and that is why, if you wish to help others, you must work first of all on purifying yourself, on sanctifying yourself. It is very difficult, but it is worthwhile, and you will be rewarded a thousandfold!

The Bonfin, 29th August, 1966

Notes

1. See *Life Force,* Complete Works, vol. 5, chap. 11: 'Peace', and *Cosmic Moral Law,* Complete Works, vol. 12, chap. 5: 'The Law of Affinity: Peace'.
2. See *'Au commencement était le Verbe' – commentaires des Évangiles,* Complete Works, vol. 9, chap. 8: 'La haute retraite'.
3. See *Boire l'élixir de la vie immortelle,* Fascicule n° 5: 'La respiration'.

Chapter Seven

THE MAGIC OF TRUSTING

To complete our discussions of the last few days on purity, I will add a few words on how to distinguish pure thoughts and feelings from impure ones. Actually, it is the magic aspect of purity that we should examine, to me as you know this is the most important aspect of any subject. But if humans refuse to accept the fact that magic exists and affects their lives and all existence, they will never come close to the Truth. They study things from the aspect of economics, aesthetics, mechanics, chemistry and physics, the social, astrological and all the other aspects, but never the magic aspect. It is the most important.[1]

A husband and wife, a professor and his students, a boss and his employees, sooner or later allow doubt and suspicion to enter their relationships: the husband notices that his wife comes home late from time to time and, without any proof, he suspects her of infidelity. Sometimes it is the wife who is tormented by jealousy and torments her husband in return, each destroying the other because they allow themselves to entertain and express the impure thoughts and feelings of their lower nature. Or it is the boss who suspects one of his employees of secretly working for a rival firm, or the employee who suspects the boss of exploiting him or spying on him... doubt and suspicion, always doubt and suspicion! What is the magic effect of all this doubt and suspicion? No one knows or cares, they find it normal and natural to suspect and torment each other with their distrust. I am not saying that you should never suspect anyone, but that you should be conscious of the forces you release when you do, and know what results to expect.

As I so often tell you, human beings have two natures, one higher and one lower. The effect, the influence you have on someone depends on which nature you appeal to, which forces you awaken. By suspecting him, you link yourself to his lower nature, not only reinforcing it, but receiving its currents yourself. When you see nothing but faults and failings in others, you open the door to those faults and failings, thus retarding your own progress, your evolution.[2]

By having in mind all the time the vices and crimes of your enemy (your neighbour, your husband) you attract the evil entities that live in him, and it should not surprise you to find yourself invaded by these evil entities. That is the magic aspect. And the opposite exists also, if you never think about the person's shortcomings but concentrate on his virtues, his spirit, whether you realize it or not a current is established between you, and if you keep on this way, one day you will resemble him. All truly great beings have known this law of osmosis, the fusion that occurs when you concentrate on someone, and for that reason they tried to be near only highly evolved beings. This is the intelligent way to think. Stupid and weak people who are interested in other people's ugliness and weaknesses do not know what they are provoking. My God, it is sad, so sad, not to be able to make humans realize that! They like gossip and scandal, they need crime stories, they cannot exist without filth. Rare are those who seek out beings who are pure, noble, wise and knowing such as the Initiates, the Masters, the Saints.

I will point out another phenomenon that you haven't noticed: by being suspicious of someone, you push that person without meaning to into doing the very thing you suspect him of! A husband suspects his wife of being unfaithful with so and so: actually it is not true, she protests, she tries to justify her actions but to no avail, the husband is mad with jealousy and makes distressing accusations. What is the result? The wife who has never asked for anything but to be faithful forever, finds herself betraying her husband, and no one is more astonished than she! It is beyond her comprehension! What made her commit adultery? It was her husband! He created the favourable conditions on the astral plane by relentlessly accusing her and she succumbed without really intending to. An ignorant husband can put an honest wife in the very situation he dreads, and the same for the husband who has to listen all day to charges of doing this, doing that, until in the end, he does it! Words create the reality.

In this way, men and women unconsciously incite good or evil in each other. This psychic phenomenon, this magic... is it so difficult to understand? People are odd, they understand higher mathematics, electronics and other complicated things, but truth, clear and simple enough for a child to grasp, they cannot understand.

That is why I want to give men and women, employers and employees, students, professors, and everyone else, a wonderful method that is sure and certain, so that instead of having doubt and suspicions about each other eternally, they may be absolutely sure. To live a whole life based on supposition, with no proof, is stupid... at least have proof! And the best proof is to say to yourself, 'I am done with doubting, now I want to be certain, to know (Hurrah! At least you want to know, which is a step above supposing, doubting, and poisoning the whole world). Since I know that my mind is blind and I must not trust it entirely, I will develop intuition and become clairvoyant.' And then you work on concentration, you meditate, pray, fast and so on... until forty or fifty years later, you become clairvoyant... at last you know for sure whether your wife is betraying you or not!

Do not laugh, dear brothers and sisters, at least with this method you will be certain! You say, 'It takes too long!' It takes time, but it is worth it: you will be clairvoyant. Otherwise in fifty or sixty years you will still not know for sure, you will reach the end of your life and die without being sure of anything. It is a serious matter, you see, and I am giving you the answer, the solution: in the end, everything leads to the development of spiritual faculties, even ignorance and doubt!

So that you will know what will happen to you, I will tell you a story. Once upon a time there was a king who went for a walk in the country and came upon a cow, a beautiful cow (her adorable shape, spots and colour, etc., were such that he practically fell in love with her). Now the cow belonged to an old wise man. When the king sent one of his followers with an order to give the cow to the king, the wise man answered, 'No. I will not give away my cow, I need her myself.' The king flew into a temper when he was given the answer, and exclaimed, 'Well then, we will seize the cow by force!' and sent several armed men to seize the cow. The wise man, who was actually the most learned and eminent personage in the kingdom, simply held out his hand in the direction of the armed men and paralysed them on the spot. When they revived, he sent them away. Then the king sent his entire army to fetch the cow, but the sage held out his hand again, and the army was paralysed and dismissed. The king was very unhappy, especially at being humiliated. 'No one has ever affronted me like this,' he said. 'Everyone obeys me. This old fellow is the first one to dare to oppose me. I will not give in, when I want something, I get it.' And he thought for a long time. 'Since that is the way it is,' he thought, 'I will go in disguise and ask him to teach me the secret of his power. Once I have learned his secret, I will know how to paralyse people myself and I will take his cow away from him!' He sought out the sage and bowed before him. 'Sir Sage,' he said. 'I salute you. Your fame has spread throughout the kingdom: I would like to become your disciple. Will you accept me?' The sage recognized the king and read his thoughts. 'Yes,' he replied. 'I accept. Come! I will reveal my secrets to you and you too will be invincible.' The king was very proud and happy. For years he worked on the exercises he was given, night and day he meditated and purified himself until he became so enlightened, so wise and so evolved that he no longer had any desire for the cow, he had forgotten her!

That is what will happen to you once you have found purity and light. When you have real force, you will no longer want to know whether your wife has betrayed you or not, nor whether your Master is a charlatan... you will even be ashamed of having spent so much time and thought on such useless things, you will be like the king and you will let the cow be. You say, 'But fifty years is a long time!' It may be sixty, or ninety... but what difference does it make? The important thing is to become sure and certain. Wouldn't it be worth it, to be always sure?

Initiates have to be sure, they cannot let themselves suspect and doubt. If you think I waste time on suppositions! No, since the very beginning I have always trusted people, I have been confident and sure that I could trust them. I know that destiny is against many of them, but I also know that if I give them a little credit, some capital symbolically speaking, they will open a shop and earn enough not only to return my loan but they will have enough left to give to others! They will do what I did for them, give others a chance to pick themselves up and solve their problems. If God never gave credit, no one would survive. I try to do as He does. Many people, poor unfortunate people, have come to see me, and I trusted them; most have gone to work and come back later to pay me what I advanced in the way of credit. Unless you give people credit and trust them, they will go on wading around in the shallows forever.

Nothing can work without confidence. To take your car out of the garage, only that, requires confidence in all the other drivers you will meet, and if you are thinking, 'Ah, that one is going to hit me, that driver doesn't know how to drive, what will he do next?' and so on, you will be in trouble all the time and not get anywhere. Confidence is absolutely indispensible to make things work. If you think I cannot see what is written on people's faces in the way of vice, etc.! I may have no intuition or clairvoyance, but I have studied physiognomy, and... I will not tell you what I see. I never do, I keep it to myself. My secret is to give everyone credit, and this confidence enables me to get things done... how could I have started this Brotherhood if I had been suspicious of everyone? But no one wants to think that way, no one else realizes that trust awakens the divine in people.[3]

If you have confidence in someone, even if he is vicious, even if he is weak, even if he is a drunk, the confidence you show him will urge him to prove that you were not wrong in your appraisal, that he is as fine and noble as you thought... that he can in fact be trusted. Even a criminal will succeed in reforming if you show confidence in him. It is a power that disarms others, but you have no desire for that power. It is true that confidence can occasionally get you into trouble, but compared to all the good things confidence brings you, it is worth the risk. In a case full of apples and pears, you know that some will be rotten, but does that make you throw out the case? Among all the people I have trusted, some have done me great harm it is true, but many more have rewarded my trust a thousandfold.

People who do not understand this magic are reserved, haughty, suspicious, severe, and pass for intelligent. No one dares bite them, but no one loves them either. Isn't it better to be bitten and stung, but in the end to gain the whole world? The few who are not worthy will betray you, no one knows that better than I, but does the fact that people exist who are weak, selfish, cruel and ungrateful mean that we should despise all mankind?

No, dear brothers and sisters, that is not a good philosophy; people who think that way do so out of ignorance. If they had any knowledge of human nature, if they believed in the magic of certain laws, then in spite of all kinds of trouble, injustice, cruelty, accidents and betrayal, they would go on being confident and trusting, enlightening others and helping them to find happiness by revealing Nature's wonderful treasures to them. One day those who have tried to harm you will come to you weeping bitter tears and begging forgiveness for having been against their greatest benefactor. Yes, when they see how ignobly they have behaved, they will want to go and hide. Once I understood that, I chose to go on having confidence, love and patience; even with those who are already digging my grave, I go on being kind and giving the best of myself.

Actually, no one is as ruthless as an Initiate, his is the greatest revenge of all. Seeing that the means of revenge used by everyone else, weapons or cruel words, obtain no results,[4] he uses another means to get back at his enemy. His revenge is to give ceaselessly to others, to feed and enlighten them, and one day, they realize how ungrateful and ignoble they have been and are unconsolable. People have come to me in tears, yes, weeping, because of all the things they had done to persecute me, whilst I, knowing what they were doing, went on bringing them the light, bringing them closer to Heaven. No one can resist that form of revenge! I congratulate myself at having found a way to win a real victory. It will not be possible, possible, believe me, for humans to keep on resisting forever. When they see you growing stronger spiritually whilst they grow more and more ravaged by poison and impurity, they can only see how far they have fallen.

I will disclose still another law: people who live in inner ugliness and darkness, see nothing but ugliness and darkness around them. This is an absolute formula, a law to remember. People who are dishonest, grasping, wily, crooked, unjust, do not believe that honest, straight, just and kind people exist, they judge the world according to the way they are themselves. And those who have fine qualities cannot see any wickedness, cruelty or treachery in others, they see everyone in the light of their own qualities. That is the law. I have met people who cannot see dishonesty or evil in others no matter how wicked, and I have met others who do not believe that anyone on earth can be exceptionally fine. Man sees through his own eyes, he is the one who forms his eyes by his thinking and by his feelings. People who are always talking about other people's faults and failings, you can be sure have those faults and failings themselves, because if they were fine and noble and kind and loving, they would think that everyone else was that way too.

In proof, why is it that all mothers think their children are angelic and divine? They see through the eyes of their love, and love is blind! Actually, the child may not be angelic, he may be a complete rascal, but to his mother he is an angel. A girl in love thinks the object of her love is beautiful, poetic, a god, until the day she becomes irritated with him, and then her disillusionment makes her see him as a monster, the devil incarnate. All of a sudden! Yesterday he was divine, today he is a monster. Does anyone change so radically in one day? No, her thoughts are what changed, people are what we think they are, we see them through our eyes, according to our ability to see.

Leave the others alone, let them be. That is what I do. I let the brothers and sisters do what they like and even if it is something wrong, I do not bother to punish them... I say to myself that others who sent them here on earth will do that, it is their business to rap them on the knuckles or take away certain advantages, not mine. I am here to do my work, not to judge, but to enlighten you. If I wished, I could summon you one by one, stand you in front of a mirror and say, 'See this or that mark on your face? It proves that you have such and such a weakness, such and such a vice. You may fool the rest of the world, but you cannot fool me.' Why not do it? Because it is not my business, others are there to do that sort of thing. I know that I allow people to stay on when all they do is slide backwards and I should say to them, 'Be off, the door is closed to you here.' But I do not, I accept everyone and close the door only to those who are dangerous, really dangerous for the Brotherhood. As long as they present no threat to the Brotherhood I let them stay, because I know that Divine Justice will handle the situation.

You see, dear brothers and sisters, unless I describe my intentions and my methods, you will not understand my way of acting. I want it all to be clear for you. Why do I pretend not to see what you do in secret? Because I would be the loser! You can concentrate on what is wrong with others if you wish, but you will see what the results are. As for me, I will go on noticing only your higher Self, the divine in you, I will do everything I can to liberate that side and feed and nourish that side, and when I win, all Heaven will be mine! In my head there is a scientific plan that I go by, I know what I am doing. Otherwise I would do as the world does. But thanks to all I know, thanks to the Light God has given me, I pay attention only to what is marvelous. Couldn't you do the same?

If you wish Heaven to have confidence in you, never open your ears or your soul to the gossip you hear. Say, 'Look, not now, not here in a Divine School, there are so many better things to do than that! Why throw dirt on each other? Why not leave all that behind now?' But what you say is, 'Oh, tell me, tell me!' And you feed on filth as if you really needed that nourishment! Unfortunately that is the case, you do still need it. What do people do when they are together... praise God? Commune with the angels? No, they feed each other's lowest appetites, that is why they are together. And when they have told all the disgusting, infernal stories they know, they are happy! Extraordinary, this need to chew at each other... we are not vegetarians, we are carnivores! Flesh eaters, feeding on entrails and fresh blood! Yes, that's it, symbolically. And we think we are spiritual!

Why do you force me to say these negative and unpleasant things? It doesn't make me happy, I would far rather talk about the divine and beautiful side of human nature, my whole being leans toward the good, the pure, the luminous in life. I also know there is danger in stressing the importance of negative things if only for a moment, afterwards I wash thoroughly: talking about them makes me feel as though I had been through a sewer.

If people were at least sure of what they say! But no, they discuss everyone without proof, and this is really not honest, nor noble, nor just... you shouldn't tolerate it, you should say, 'Show me a proof of what you are saying or else shut up.' But I have found the answer: go to Tibet or somewhere, and find a great sage. Then instead of wondering whether your wife is unfaithful or not, your Master an impostor or not, or if so and so might not be a thief, an assassin... spend fifty years learning the spiritual disciplines. In the end you will be so great, so high-minded and noble that you will forget all the rest. If you are lacking in intuition, go somewhere and develop it, but don't listen to your poor intellect, always doubting, always the cause of trouble, yours and the whole world's. Look at how many tragedies are the result of doubt and suspicion! And don't let me hear you say that I have not had confidence in the Brotherhood! For years I have had nothing else!

You don't realize that one day you will be called upon to appear before the shining beings of the invisible world who will say to you, 'We are the ones who spoke through your Master, why did you not believe what he said? Do you know how great a debt you owe? Billions!' And they will present you with a bill. The law is implacable: you have received, you must give. You say, 'Do you mean we are to give money?' No, I am not asking for you to give money or anything else, only one day you will be obliged to do for others as much as has been done for you. Yes, dear brothers and sisters, one day you will have to show to others the same selflessness, the same abnegation, indulgence and love that you have received... in that way you pay your debt. That is justice.

I too have received much. The invisible world took me in charge and still has me in charge, enlightening me, teaching and helping me. I owe a tremendous debt for this grace, these blessings and abundance and love that I receive night and day. How will I pay this debt? By working for the invisible world, paving the way so that God's plans can be realized. And you, do you think you can escape your obligations? How ignorant you are! One day you will have to pay. You should not have gone to the restaurant, symbolically speaking, but you did, you ate, and now, it is written: you must pay. Is it not better to pay and be able to keep coming to this restaurant? Yes, it is. Stones do not have to pay, but they remain stones! Unless you would prefer that? The law is implacable, when you receive, you must give. You have received freely, you must give freely.[5]

I would like you to understand today once and for all that you must be done with doubt and suspicion. As I say, I do not bother with uncertainty, even where you are concerned. I do not ask myself whether you are good or bad, pure or degenerate, intelligent or stupid, I know. I am never in doubt. If someone came and told me terrible things about you, do you think I would believe them automatically, just like that? No, I would verify what was said, I would invite you to come and see me, I would observe you and ask you questions and listen to your answers. Actually I use three things. First I use my intuition, I ask the beings in the invisible world to tell me what they think above; then I use my knowledge of physiognomy; thirdly, I might take a glance at your horoscope. Then I will be certain. You don't even know how to start investigating, that is the sad thing.

When you know something, know it once and for all! 'But that is not the way it is... I thought I saw... I couldn't see...' To you, things are always vague and uncertain, fogbound. I want to take you away from that and bring you to the land of certainty. People say, 'This person is a drunk... that one is dishonest.' I take a look at the person in question for the face is revealing,

I look at his hands, the way he walks, I listen to his voice, for that is where a man betrays himself even if he is good at hiding things. I do not bother with his carefully studied attitudes, his affectations so carefully worked out. No, I will look at the almost imperceptible, unconscious movements he makes with his mouth, his nose, his eyes, his fingers. People forget details, no one can hide themselves completely. Only when you don't know what to look for can you be fooled. The tiniest detail is revealing, but most people don't know what to look for; as they never study themselves, they don't even know when they are betraying themselves.

Examine people who spend their time spreading doubt and lies and suspicion about others: perhaps (in the case of a woman), she wanted to be married or have a lover and was not able to, and invented all kinds of unbelievable stories accusing others of doing what she was not able to do. This is called being repressed, a condition familiar to psychoanalysts. The sad thing is that everyone believes the poor creature! Instead of making sure, of verifying things, of studying the person's walk, his weight, his look, the colour of his skin or his horoscope to see if this aggressiveness does not come from a conjunction of the Moon and Mars, for instance... everyone takes joy in believing everything that is said! No one has any knowledge of physiognomy, no intuition to help them in their judgments. In these circumstances, even if the greatest Initiate came down on earth, no one would benefit from his presence, he would always be suspect.

Sometimes men talk about how awful their wives are; if I believed them, there would be no one left! When I summon the wife in question however, what do I discover? The husband is the one who is awful, a monster, and she, his victim! Or wives come complaining about their husbands, but when I see the husband, I find that he is a poor miserable fellow, and his wife is a shrew, and not tamed either! Believe me, dear brothers and sisters, do not be in such a hurry to pronounce yourselves. Study the situation and then, if you must, state your opinion. But first of all, wait; have the patience to look into the matter.

All this to make you understand that doubt, gossip, suspicion, are impurities. The proof is that you are poisoned by them. Anyone who wants to purify himself must be done with all those things and put confidence, trust, love, and especially an impersonal attitude, unselfishness, in their place. Those who always have a personal interest and seek some advantage, pick up all the impurities on the astral plane, whereas those who work for a divine ideal are purified by it night and day. The ideal itself purifies them.

We think that purity comes from not looking at women, not touching them. You can look at them, walk and talk with them and not ever be soiled in any way, but only if you are disinterested, if you are not personally involved. Purity does not lie in avoiding women, looking down at the ground as the religious advocated in the past. For a long time I have been disgusted with this way of thinking about purity and saintliness that we were given centuries ago, it is not the way I think. I feel free to change and upset those notions, because I have nothing to hide. I realize that if the sages prescribed this attitude in the past they had their reason, even if they were pure and strong enough to be sure of themselves, they had to be careful of others without that control who might be disturbed or tempted. There was a reason for their prescriptions, but the same methods shouldn't be made to last forever, other more modern, more psychological methods must be found for today.

I know that my attitude will shock some people: when they see that I do not conform to the ancient traditions, they will suspect me. But those traditions are no more than form, appearances. I could conform to them and fool the whole world, living in secret anyway I please and outwardly presenting a spotless appearance. How many people do that, knowing that people look only at appearances, how many outwardly respect forms and inwardly indulge in immorality? I do not care about appearances, if you haven't enough intuition or clairvoyance to sense how pure someone's life is, well, I don't need you. I know brothers and sisters who surpass the outward forms and traditions and go much further as far as purity is concerned. Even if there are only two or three like that, never mind, I will do the work with them.

Most humans do not know what true morality, true purity, is. They make citations, they preach conventional forms, but life does not come flowing out of them. Purity is not in form, nor in citations, purity is in the intensity of thought and feeling, that is, in the intensity of one's spiritual life. That is purity.

Yes, to all who have remained true to the old traditions, I say, 'O all you sainted ones, you chaste and noble perfections, why is it that you are always upset, always complaining of disharmony, discouragement and illness? How is it that your purity has done so little for you? You who think of yourself as the summit of purity, are you any better than you were? No. Well, then, what kind of purity is that? True purity brings everything else along with it. Why are you weak, why are you afraid, worried and anxious, why are you so ignorant? Is that what your kind of purity has done for you?' If they are honest, they will lower their heads, and begin to understand. No creature on earth has as much reverence as I for all truly pure, chaste creatures. But a purity that makes people mediocre, my God, that is not what I am looking for! Purity as I understand it, is the beginning of everything, the foundation, the base of everything, *Yesod,* as the Kabala calls it.

The Bonfin, 20th August, 1966

Notes

1. See *The Book of Divine Magic,* Izvor Coll. n° 226, chap. 10: 'We All Work Magic'.

2. See *Aux sources inaltérables de la joie,* Izvor Coll. n° 242, chap. 13: 'Nos relations avec les autres reflètent notre degré d'évolution'.

3. See *Love Greater Than Faith,* Izvor Coll. n° 239, chap. 10: 'Base your trust on vigilance'.
4. See *Love and Sexuality,* Complete Works, vol. 15, chap. 27: 'Our Only Weapons: Love and Light'.
5. See *'Cherchez le Royaume de Dieu et sa Justice'*, Synopsis Coll., Part VII, chap. 4-II: 'Notre dette envers le Créateur, la création et les créatures'.

Chapter Eight

PURITY OF SPEECH

There is the story of the man who went to Mohammed and said, 'I have done something wrong, I have accused a friend of something he did not do, I lied, and now I am unhappy because I don't know what I can do to repair things. What should I do?' Mohammed answered, 'I will tell you what to do: go and place a feather in front of every house in the city and then come back here to me.' The man went and did as he was told, he left a feather on every doorstep of every house throughout the city and then came back. 'Very good,' said Mohammed. 'Now go and pick up all the feathers and bring them here to me.' A few hours later the man reappeared saying, 'There is not a single feather left, Sir Prophet, I cannot find a single feather.' Then Mohammed said to him, 'Now you know what happens to words, they escape, they fly away like feathers: you can never get them back.' The man went away more miserable than ever.

I would have added something more to that advice. If someone asked me how to repair an injury, a false accusation, gossip or slander, I would tell him this, 'Now go and talk again about the same person, this time enumerating his good qualities and virtues, his kindness, his good intentions... you can always find something good to talk about if you look for it.' Will this absolve you from the fault you committed? No, it is too late:

the words you pronounced have already reached their mark in the invisible regions, perhaps even in the visible regions, and had their effect. But by your subsequent words you will create a different effect that will compensate for the earlier one and when the Karma you incurred comes to collect, you will be obliged to pay of course, but right on the heels of that Karma will come the result of your good words, and that will be your consolation....

What are words? Words are rockets that go off in space and release all kinds of forces. In the case of harmful words, they excite entities and cause irreparable damage.[1] Yes, irreparable. The effect may be less terrible if you make immediate repairs, but the more time goes by, the more damage there will be. 'Even if I say the contrary afterwards?' Your good words will be rewarded, but you will still have to pay for the others, that is, receive the effects they incurred. People do not realize this, they think they can say anything they like, but no, dear brothers and sisters, once spoken the good and bad words we speak go to separate regions and are buried under terrestrial or supra-terrestrial layers. That is why they can never be retrieved. You see why time is essential. Suppose you have issued the order to cut off someone's head. What can you do once the executioner has carried out your order and the head is severed from its shoulders, can you stick it back on? Nothing can be done once the order is carried out. You might try sending another order to stop the execution, but it will be useless if too much time has elapsed. *'Let not the sun go down on thy wrath... if thou hast aught against thy brother, before the sun set...'* means that we should not put off trying to repair the damage we have done to others by our sins and transgressions, because Karma, or justice, acts instantly and we will be obliged to pay down to the last penny. Most people do not know about the law of Karma, they let their feelings boil over and say what they like about each other, but sooner or later Karma knocks on the door and says, 'Pay!' You have to do something at once because words fly off into space and become a tremendously active force... for good or for evil.

There is another power even more active and effective than speech, which is thought: if you act immediately in thought, you can overtake the unfortunate words you have uttered... it is difficult, because speech and thought belong to different regions. Speech is vibration, displaced air, and belongs on the physical plane; thought is etheric and belongs on a higher plane. If you beseech the invisible world mentally to repeal the consequences of your harmful words, it may not be completely effective, but you will avoid the worst. Your thought must be very intense and very rapid for the order to be canceled... otherwise the victim will be decapitated (symbolically) and you will be held responsible.

People imagine it is enough to be forgiven by the person they have wronged, but the damage must also be repaired, only then will they be free. It is not enough to say, 'Excuse me, I am so sorry...' You say thank you when you receive a gift, but is 'thank you' the equivalent of the gift? 'Excuse me' is not enough... if you have set fire to someone's house, it is not enough to excuse yourself, you must build him a new house, only then will you deserve real forgiveness. You say, 'But what if the person I have harmed forgives me?' No, it is not that easy, the person and the law are two different things. The law does not forgive until you have made reparation in full.

Of course, the person who forgives shows that he is noble and generous, he is in the process of disengaging himself and becoming free of all the suffering that holds him back in the lower regions. A person who does not forgive goes on suffering, his thoughts are bound and held by the image of the person who wronged him, he thinks of nothing else, and this keeps him from advancing. When Jesus said to forgive our enemies, it was so that man could be liberated from all the negative thoughts, the rancour and vengeful feelings that gnaw at him and ultimately destroy him.[2] This is the extraordinary law. Forgiveness on the part of the one who has been hurt leads to liberation for himself, but not for the one who injured him... that person must make amends before he can be free.

When you lie about someone and slander him, you ruin his prestige, his honour, which leads to distressing events that may even block his evolution. If you go and ask him to forgive you and he does, he is liberated, but as you have done nothing to make reparation, the lies you spread (the snakes and tigers and wolves that devour him symbolically) are still there and even devour his young lambs... meaning that your words also affect his family or friends, making matters all the worse for you. You must seek and find the right words, the thoughts and forces that will repair the damage you have done. Then you will be forgiven both by the person you wronged and by the law. Excuses do no good as far as you are concerned, they may help the injured person who is seeking liberation, but they settle nothing from the point of view of justice.

The Teaching explains certain things to help you to mend your ways consciously. If you have a tendency (as everyone has) to anger, bitterness, cruelty, or a critical attitude, you can then do something about it. To have such tendencies is normal but if knowledge is available that will enable you to correct them, then you should avail yourself of it. A lot of people do nothing about correcting their faults, they are even rather proud of their audacity and vulgarity, which makes it all the more serious, for they will never repair the harm they do... when Karma comes looking for them, no one, absolutely no one, will be able to help. Even Jesus could not save John the Baptist, for his Karma was too heavy. John the Baptist was the Prophet Elias in an earlier incarnation, and he cut off the heads of four hundred and fifty false prophets, worshippers of Baal. There was no excuse for this crime and he had to pay by having his own head cut off in a later incarnation.[3] Jesus said to Peter in the Garden of Gethsemani, *'Put up thy sword into its place for they that take the sword shall perish with the sword.'* Even Jesus could not save John the Baptist.

When people feel a need to humiliate and browbeat others, it is generally because their own lives are difficult, they lack money or other advantages and take out their resentment on the rest of the world. They would do better to go and weep in a corner and leave others alone... not only because the Karma they create by their destructive attitude will be relentless in extracting payment from them, but because harmful words stir up a force that is harmful to others. That is not allowed, you must know that.

One must be conscious of the danger of giving in to one's bad tendencies and realize that they are a weakness rather than something to be proud of. Destructive and harmful forces can only be controlled by surveying and controlling oneself all the time, not by thinking that everything one does is marvellous. If someone came along with the same destructive tendencies and crushed you the way you crush others, you would not think he had any reason for pride. You must realize that when you are tough, overbearing or gross, someone will come along to deal with you who is even tougher, more overbearing, and grosser than you.

The law of correspondences, the law of affinity, is one of Nature's most remarkable and powerful laws. Thoughts and feelings are determined, their specific nature corresponds with forces in space of the same nature: good thoughts and feelings attract good forces and consequently good results; bad, hurtful thoughts and feelings attract harmful forces and bad results. That is the law of affinity. Initiates counsel us to love one another, because they know that we will then be loved in return: when you love, you awaken the forces of love in the universe and loving forces come crowding in on you so that you think, 'What have I ever done for the good Lord to deserve so much love?' You have spread loving thoughts and automatically the

good forces created by them are drawn to you and go to work
for you. The same is true for hatred, of course, destructive
thoughts come back as a destructive force... against you. The
world is ignorant, these things are unknown to humans, and
consequently they are always in trouble.

You should know that when you say something against
someone, the only way to make repairs is to start praying
immediately and to send that person a great deal of love and
light. Even then, a certain amount of damage is inevitable,
it takes time for good thoughts to take effect. The words of
Mohammed are profoundly true, thoughts like feathers fly away
and cannot be retrieved. Only by projecting good, positive
forces will there be beneficial results; if you project negative,
destructive forces, there will be destructive results. In this way
good and evil coexist, but on two separate levels. Evil produces
evil, and good produces good.

Suppose you have a field in which you sow wheat and tares
at the same time: both will grow, the earth feeds every seed that
is planted irrespective of whether it is good or bad. It won't
do any good to say that the earth is stupid to do that and that
she should starve the bad seeds, she will only answer, 'I don't
understand what you mean, I am to nourish and protect every
single seed, to me all seeds are good, even the bad ones are
potentially good.' And Nature says the same: when you plant
wonderful ideas, you know that the harvest will be wonderful;
and when your ideas are evil, Nature will nourish and strengthen
them just as if they were good. You see, the bad has as much
right to survive as the good. Until when? Until the harvest.
When the time comes for the harvest, the owner of the field can
choose to throw the bad lot into the fire and store the wheat in
the loft. Jesus said this,[4] he knew that evil has every right to
grow along with the good, that it is up to man not to plant evil
in the first place. Is that clear now?

Those who spent time in past incarnations working on their
virtues and developing artistic or scientific faculties, return in

the next incarnation with the harvest, the fruit of that work: they have sown, they have planted, and now they are gifted. There is a story about a young man who came to ask Mozart for advice on how to compose a symphony. Mozart said to him, 'But you are young: you should start with minuets.' 'What,' said the young man. 'I am young? What about you, you began composing symphonies at the age of twelve!' 'Yes,' said Mozart. 'But I did not need advice.' That shows you the difference between people who have worked in their preceding incarnations and those who have not!

You say, 'But what is the connection between purity and words?' Must I really answer that question? Words that come from the soul and spirit are inspired by beautiful, selfless and impartial thoughts, words that are pure in that they awaken only divine thoughts and feelings in others, never anything destructive. Words can have a cleansing, purifying effect on people, they can flow like a river, a torrent that makes everything in its path clear and pure; or words can do the opposite if such is their nature, and soil people. It requires constant meditation to confine oneself to words that cleanse and purify human hearts. Yes, how does one purify people whose appetites and desires are crude and gross? Words can do it, but only if they come from above.

Remember what I have said today about words and, God willing, we will continue during the coming days to discuss purity. For purity is a most formidable science. Everything is based on purity, the purity of a look, the purity of words, of gestures, of thought, of feelings, of intention, purity makes a man divine! The trouble is, there are not many who realize how important purity is. Only the Initiates really seek it because they know that if they do not live in intense purity, they will never get anywhere. Public opinion does not count for them, what counts for an Initiate is to be pure before Heaven, and that is what he works toward night and day... what others think of him is immaterial. What is public opinion? If a man is impure, can public opinion make him pure? And if he is pure, he cannot ever be blackened regardless of public opinion.

And so, dear brothers and sisters, you too must decide to work on purity so that all together we can become a great radiating power in the world, dispensing light to clean and purify the atmosphere of the whole world. No work is more glorious than that. If you are looking for real glory, divine glory, you should plunge yourself in this work and, whatever the opinion of others, be a source of living water that purifies everything around you. What is the work of a cabinet minister, a general or a president compared to the grandeur of this work? Nothing. I must tell you this, because you are often unable to discern what activities to devote your life to.

Men usually choose the activity that will bring them the most money or the most prestige, they want to be served rather than to serve. Jesus said, *'Whosoever will be chief among you, let him be your servant.'* To be a servant means to purify creatures, to remove the dirt that has accumulated in their minds and hearts. Whoever wants to start out by being great is doomed to remain small, the more time goes by the more he diminishes, until no one pays attention to him, he is forgotten. It was his ignorance that betrayed him, he should have been content to be small at the beginning, that is, a servant. When you have served others for a long time, they finally realize what you have done for them, they come and ask to be your servants, and you become their master! You refuse, but they insist, they even entreat you to rule them. Again you refuse. Finally they take you by force and set you on the throne, place a crown on your head and call you their ruler. What else can you do but rule? But for such a thing to happen, you must have been willing for a long time, a very long time, to be no more than a servant.

The Bonfin, 1st September, 1966

Notes
1. See *The Fruits of the Tree of Life – The Cabbalistic Tradition,* Complete Works, vol. 32, chap. 11: 'The Living Logos'.
2. See *'Au commencement était le Verbe' – commentaires des Évangiles,* Complete Works, vol. 9, chap. 9: 'Père, pardonne-leur car ils ne savent ce qu'ils font'.
3. See *Man, Master of his Destiny,* Izvor Coll. n° 202, chap. 8: 'Reincarnation'.
4. See *Spiritual Alchemy,* Complete Works, vol. 2, chap. 8: 'The Parable of the Tares'.

Chapter Nine

TO FIND PURITY

If a man is not pure, he will have obstacles to meet with on his path, stones to trip over, thorns to prick his flesh, broken glass to make his feet bleed, impediments of all kinds to slow him down. Purity clears the way, but humans do not bother with purity, they think they can live without it. Maybe so, but for how long?

When you have trouble seeing clearly, when your thoughts are muddled, it is because you have accumulated impurities that block your vision, as if you lived near a well-traveled highway with cars and people constantly stirring up clouds of dust... or near a swamp filled with stagnant water that fills the air with mist and vapours. In order to see clearly, you must go above the dust and the mist.

Dust symbolizes the average mind, always agitated, always bargaining and negotiating questionable deals. Fog symbolizes the vague, hazy feelings of the astral plane. The lower mental plane is covered with dry dust, the lower astral plane is hidden in the mist of passion and senseless effervescence. The work of a disciple consists in rising above those planes through meditation, prayer, contemplation, removing himself from all dust and fog in order to gain a clear view.

People who are absorbed in the tumult of ordinary occupations, discussions, arguments, business dealings, have no time to go to the higher regions and see what the world looks like from above. There you see the beginning and the end of things, you observe the structure of the universe and enjoy utter clarity. Do you want to be free, above everything that might hamper your progress, dependent on no one? Then go above the clouds. As long as you remain below, you are at the mercy of the clouds: if they choose not to let the sun through, then you have to remain huddled in the shadows, shivering with cold, waiting for them to disperse. When they move on you feel better, of course, but is that being free?

Initiates do not wait for the clouds to break up, they go above them to where the sun shines all the time and they can warm themselves in its light. If you wait for favourable circumstances, you might have to wait for years, for your whole life, and even go to the other side without ever experiencing a day in the light, or ever finding out what life really is. In Bulgaria they say, 'He came in as a calf and left as a bull,' meaning that he changed in size only, not in his thinking, and was still a member of the bovine family at the end of his life.

Initiates, no matter what is happening in the world do not wait for it to get better, they go high up in thought into the light of the inner sun. There they find the solution to problems, the courage and inspiration they need... and even health and beauty! Whilst they are there the situation below resolves itself and they win on both planes! If you wait around for the problems to be solved, you become impatient, embittered and ill, and you miss the opportunity to advance, progress, evolve! You must wait, but whilst you wait, you work! That is the solution.

If you wait without doing anything, you lose. You can do nothing to bring a war to an end perhaps, or make the trains run if there is a strike, but you can do more than tear your hair out! Oh, I know you will always find things to do, you run around complaining, or rob a bank, or kill someone... yes, you know how to be agitated, only agitation does not have much effect in the higher regions, it may even be considered an impediment.

Here, you are taught how to work, what to do under every circumstance, and especially, how to go above and release the real forces in the region of the mind and spirit.[1]

You have flown in a plane, have you not? The extraordinary experience of being above the clouds in the pure sky and brilliant sunlight while below the world is hidden from view, demonstrates the importance of going higher up. When you are below the sun is hidden by the clouds, and without the sun, the sky is dark, you are cold and lacking in energy. Compare spring and summer with winter: in winter, when there is less light, animals lie down in their shelters and sleep, trees lose their foliage, rivers stop flowing, peasants stop working and light the fire. Of course in towns and cities life goes on at the same rapid pace summer or winter, but that is not Nature's rhythm.

You must learn to read the Living Book of Nature which I am always referring to, so that you too can understand and interpret it. On the mountain peaks there is never any dust, only snow... a page taken from the Book of Nature! But you never see the connection between things, you never apply Nature's laws to the mental or psychic levels.[2]

Suppose the world is suddenly plunged in a war, disaster strikes and everyone is distraught. If you climb as high as you can above the turmoil, you will see that in spite of all that is going on in the world you are in the light, filled with joy and love, an immense love which you pour out onto all suffering people. Yes, you are above the clouds and they stayed below at the mercy of circumstance. It is most important for you to get in the habit of doing this exercise every day, so that in the end you cannot live without it. In thought you go up as high as possible, all the way to the top if you can, there to discover the solution to problems and be filled with such an extraordinary feeling of beauty and riches and power that you will be at a loss for words.

Form the habit every day no matter where you are, in the street, in meetings, in the dentist's waiting room, reading, writing, singing, walking, eating, of linking yourself to the centre for a minute, the inner source, the spring flowing with sunlight, and then go back to whatever you were doing. One second is enough to form the link and then, back to work. Nothing is of greater value, nothing is more precious for your life than this habit. You say, 'But when I do it nothing happens.' No need to look for outward manifestation yet, only do the exercice: it will bring you such satisfaction, such happiness and joy, such well-being, that you will do without all the rest. In time you will become rich, strong and powerful: invulnerable! If one little exercise can give you all that joy, happiness, satisfaction, fulfilment, why ask for more? Later on you will obtain everything you want, it is merely a question of time.

As long as humans do not link themselves with the Spring, Universal Soul, and let the River of Life flow through them, they will be nothing more than slaves, bound and dependent, harassed and stepped on. My secret, the greatest and best secret, is not to work for money or glory or fame or recognition, but for the higher consciousness that will make me into a true servant of God. Once I have that I know that everything else will come, for the entire earth will follow the person who has been able to reestablish the link with Heaven.

Obviously it is a most difficult exercise, even if you do it every day it will be far from perfect, for at first only a few cells in the brain accept to go along with you and make the link, the others refuse. You must be able to convince all your cells, every part of you down to the soles of your feet.

If a mental link with Heaven was all that was needed, it would be easy, but a mental link is not enough. You must involve everyone of the reluctant, backward peoples you harbour inside... yes, there are peoples inside you, prehistoric tribes constantly fighting and devouring each other. Like the story of the remote tribe of cannibals, anthropophagans, who sent a delegation to the United Nations requesting a larger supply of missionaries because they were hungry! To convince all your inner tribes to obey you, you must talk to them and teach them incessantly, years on end, so that little by little they will learn to be obedient, even the cells below in the stomach, the intestines, the liver and spleen. If we can make all the cells in our bodies vibrate in unison, we will then be able to stir up an etheric whirlwind of fantastically powerful, far-reaching proportions.

It is not difficult to take a few cells and link them to Heaven, Christians do that when they pray, but usually the prayer goes no further than just above their heads and falls back down again. To project a prayer into space requires a lot of fuel, a lot of powder. Most of the time we haven't enough powder, that is, we mumble a prayer (which is tiring), yawn, and go to bed.

There was once a devout monk in a monastery who was given to tippling (how he tippled!) and a little bit to filching also. They were his weaknesses. Each night he said his prayers asking God to forgive him, and then he went peacefully to sleep, knowing that he was in God's good graces. He kept this up for years until by chance one night he forgot to say his prayers. In the middle of the night he felt someone shaking him and a voice said, 'Get up! You forgot to say your prayers this evening! Hurry up and say them.' Opening his eyes, he saw the Devil standing by his bed... the Devil was anxious for him to keep on praying so that he would not reform! Yes, because once he had mumbled a prayer his conscience was clear and he could begin his tippling again the next day! When the monk realized that it was the Devil who encouraged him to pray, he was so frightened he stopped drinking! They say he became a very good monk after that, and now the level of wine in the barrels no longer goes down each night. Prayers can be very good at keeping our conscience quiet so that it does not ever transform itself.

These were a few words to tell you to remember to link yourself to God every day, to do this with so much fervor, so intensely that you can no longer do without it. Whatever happens, whatever condition you find yourself in, it will be the means of getting you out of all your difficulties. Even if you end up in Hell, you will be able to get out: when the devils see you praying they will say to themselves, 'That one is going to have a bad influence on our personnel. Out with him!' And they will chase you away. If you form the habit of praying, when you find yourself in Hell you will be able to get out again.[3]

There is a story about Solomon. Finding himself on the way to Hell (no doubt over some trouble with women) somehow he managed to take a tapemeasure with him. When he arrived in Hell, he began measuring right and left, writing his calculations in a notebook. The devils ran to the head devil, 'We don't know what Solomon is doing' they cried, 'but he is up to some kind of mischief.' The head devil summoned Solomon and asked him what he was doing. 'Oh,' said Solomon. 'I am taking measurements in order to build a temple.' *'A temple,'* cried the head devil, aghast. 'Oh, my! Get out of here at once!' And Solomon was chased out of Hell. Temples are strictly forbidden in Hell you know. That is how he escaped, and if you want to do the same, I advise you to slip a tapemeasure into your vest pocket (if you are allowed in with a vest) and do as Solomon did. If it works, all the better, but if they realize that you are imitating Solomon, they will say, 'No, you don't... Not again! Once is enough... now into the kettle with you!' And you will be plunged in boiling water, but don't worry, we will come and get you out.

To attain purity, dear brothers and sisters, you must climb up as high as possible and link yourself with Heaven. Below are impurities, filth, thick mud and slime; above is transparency, clear and etheric. The purity you seek is reached by climbing up to the higher regions. Whoever learns to go higher and higher all the way to Heaven will obtain purity, he will attain it even if he is not looking for it because the very effort to rise and to surpass himself has already cleansed and purified his subtler bodies.

A piece of cloth that is to be whitened or bleached is plunged into a steaming tub. It is the same for man: when he wants to link himself with God, his higher, more subtle bodies are plunged into another atmosphere where whirlwinds and vibrations go to work and remove the stains of his errors and transgressions. Yes, there are steam baths in the higher regions from which emanate powerful vapours that purify whoever is exposed to them. If you put a handkerchief in a drawer that contains perfume, when you take it out again it emanates the perfume it is impregnated with. You too, when you go to places full of light and fragrance, are impregnated with their quintessence, with the result that you shine with light and emanate fragrance, and those who see you realize that there is something divine about you, a divine fluid emanates from you. Believe me, this is the absolute truth.

Never forget that in order to purify yourself and be able to see things clearly, what you must do is acquire the habit of climbing to the heights where the finest ideals, thoughts, feelings and desires are. A man who lets himself go sliding back down into the manure and other rotting fermentation begins to stench himself. Those who do not take care of themselves, drunks, thieves, bums... how long do you remain in their company? You hold your nose and flee! You say, 'The smell comes from cheap tobacco, or not washing, or having no new clothes to put on, doesn't it?' No. Not at all. Even if you make those people bathe, even if you clothe them in royal robes and prevent them from smoking and drinking, they will still smell, they spread the pest and contaminate you because inside they are rotten.

When men at last realize how important purity is, they will think, 'Ah, we must purify ourselves! God Almighty, I didn't realize, I plunged into the lower regions without realizing what it would do to me, and now here I am, filthy, ugly, unfit, disgusting.' And they will look for a hole to hide in. How do you explain the fact that some people prefer to be alone? Because they don't dare present themselves in public. They invent all kinds of excuses... they must be alone to write, to paint, compose, sculpt, or meditate... but they fool no one but themselves.

With animals it is instinctive to show themselves when they know they are beautiful, and the same with birds and insects. A peacock that has lost its feathers will go in hiding and wait until his feathers grow back in to show himself again. Animals know when they are fit to be admired, and show themselves or not accordingly. A child that is dressed in pretty clothes wants to be admired, but a girl who has a tiny run in her stocking will not go to a fashionable place where she might run into people, she runs home as quickly as possible. People who know they are beautiful want to show themselves and those who know they are ugly want to hide. Even the most beautiful woman in the world when she is not at her best, will refuse to go out. Her lover who is waiting, thinks she must have some important and wonderful engagement, but no, she is merely waiting for her feathers to grow back in!

You see why people whose hearts are filled with love and kindness and generosity and inner riches enjoy the company of others; they may not be handsome physically but their love and kindness make them beautiful. To want to live in society, in a collectivity, indicates that you already have at least one good quality, the love of others. If you prefer to hide in a hole by yourself, it is a very bad sign except for a genius, great artist or philosopher, or an Initiate who needs solitude for one reason: to be able to give more to mankind.

Another subject for you to reflect on, dear brothers and sisters.

The Bonfin, 2nd September, 1966

Notes

1. See *'Et il me montra un fleuve d'eau de la vie'*, Synopsis Coll., Part VIII, chap. 2: 'La maison sur le roc: le pouvoir de la pensée'.
2. See *'In Spirit and in Truth'*, Izvor Coll. n° 235, chap. 4: 'Reaching for the Top'.
3. See *La prière*, Brochure n° 305, and *Looking into the Invisible – Intuition, Clairvoyance, Dreams*, Izvor Coll. n° 228, chap. 7: 'Messages From Heaven'.

Chapter Ten

BLESSED ARE THE PURE IN HEART

When Jesus said, *'Blessed are the pure in heart for they shall see God,'* he was telling man that he must purify himself of all personal desires if he wishes to see God. To see God does not mean to see Him with physical eyesight, it means to feel His presence, to become aware of His love, His wisdom, His infinity. You ask, 'Did Jesus see God?' Jesus saw God in that he was the Christ, Christ the Son, a part of the Father. The Christ contemplates the Father because he is one with Him, made of the same substance as his Father and blended in with Him. Christ is a cosmic Spirit. If Jesus saw God, it was because he had reached identification with the Spirit of Christ, not that he saw Him with his eyes.[1]

There is much to say on this beatitude, *'Blessed are the pure in heart for they shall see God.'* To behold God requires more than the inner eye, the heart and soul: the mind and spirit must also be involved. If you have divested yourself of your base desires you will see God, that is, you will know Him as Beauty, Splendour, Infinite Space, but God Himself is so high above us that not even the pure in heart can know Him, for that you need sanctification, your spirit must be hallowed, sanctified, before you can know God. You say, 'Is he correcting the sayings of Jesus?' No, I am not correcting anything, I am simply explaining the thinking of Jesus.

The saints, prophets, apostles, martyrs, virgins and patriarchs all had pure hearts, but how many were able to see God? Even Moses, although he talked with Him, was not able to see God. That too must be interpreted. God Himself never spoke to Moses, nor to Buddha, nor to Zoroaster, nor to Orpheus. He spoke through the intermediary of His messengers, the great Archangels. No one would survive hearing the Voice of God or being in His Presence, they would be pulverized. It is only fortune tellers and mediums and so-called clairvoyants who 'see' God and converse with Him.

When I lived on the Rue des Princes in Boulogne, I occasionally ran into an old woman... I cannot describe her, it would take too many colours, too many brush strokes, but each time I met her she told me the most extraordinary tales of having seen Jesus and talked with him. So as not to hurt her feelings, I would listen. One day she told me she had planned to talk with Jesus that morning but as he was busy she had conversed with God. God obligingly filled in for Jesus... imagine! And as I was curious to see what He had talked to her about, I asked her. 'Ah!' she replied. 'I was on my way to market and God told me what to buy that day!' Is that all God has to do? He must have plenty of spare time if He can think about an old biddy and her marketing!

Old biddies are not the only ones to have a strange concept of God. Many strange occupations are attributed to Him. Why did He create thousands of Angels and Archangels (a fact we accept) if He had no need for them, nothing for them to do? What were they all doing whilst He alone created the world? During the six days were they watching God work with no effort to help Him? If they were useless why did He keep them?

No. According to the Kabala, God gave His Plan for the Creation to the seventh order of Angels, the Elohim, and they carried out that Plan. God has His servants who act as intermediaries between Him and us. If you think God listens to all the requests humans send Him and then answers them one by one!

No one has ever seen God because God is Infinite, Unlimited. You can feel His Presence, you can see His manifestations of light, the lightning for instance, but the Author of these manifestations cannot be seen, to see God is not possible, that is all there is to it! To be seen there must be dimensions, limits, a form situated somewhere in space and time: God is outside space and time, we can only perceive Him in a few scattered reflections and manifestations. When you have been before the sun you may say, 'I have seen God as Light, I have felt God as Warmth, and the result is that I am more alive,' but to say that you have seen God and talked with Him is nothing short of blasphemous.

I know that it is written in the Bible that the patriarchs and prophets talked with God. For humans to grasp Reality, truths have to be explained in a way that is within human limitations and comprehension.[2] Limited minds cannot grasp the unlimited, smallness cannot comprehend Infinity. When will humans be able to see clearly? When they become part of immensity, when they melt into space and become part of that immensity themselves, then they will have an idea of Infinity.

A drop of water separated from all the other drops that form the ocean may have the same qualities, the same composition as the ocean, but it is not part of it. If it is reabsorbed into the ocean and is no longer separate, it becomes the ocean again, and consequently *knows* the ocean. As long as man is separate from God he cannot understand immensity, the Infinite Vastness of God, he must melt into His ocean and become part of Him in order to know Him,[3] because then he *is* Him. As long as he is outside God, he cannot know Him, because by himself man is finite, limited, human. Only purification can awaken the faculties latent within him that will allow him to conceive of the Infinite. When he develops his Buddhic and his Atmic bodies and is endowed with practically unlimited possibilities, when he melts into immensity, then he will *know* the Eternal, the Infinite God.

The purity of *Yesod* will teach you how to see God.

In the *Gospels* it says, *'If thine eye be single* (pure) *thy whole body shall be full of light.'* Jesus did not say, 'If your eyes are...', but *'If thine eye is...'* From the physiological point of view this is absurd, the state of the body does not depend on the eyes but the other way round. Jesus said, *'If thine eye be single, thy whole body shall be full of light,'* because it was not the two eyes of the human body that he was thinking of but another eye: the third eye. In the effort to become pure man rids his inner eye of the thick layers that veil it, thus allowing the luminous currents coming from the divine world to enter the body and purify it. Jesus was talking about the organ or faculty called the third eye that permits one to see things as they really are, to know where they come from and thanks to this knowledge, to be able to choose.[4]

The third eye guides man, it shows him what to do, with whom to create a bond, how to act, what to accept in the way of nourishment. Thanks to being able to see clearly, thanks to this vision, he avoids introducing into his bloodstream, his soul and thoughts, all impure, harmful elements. His third eye keeps him pure. In that way the third eye can be said to act on the body. And when his eye is pure, man begins to see, to feel, to understand the truth.

I will add that anyone who wants to penetrate into the divine world without prior purification will find his way barred. The luminous beings forbid the intrusion of impure entities who contaminate everything with their miasmas and waste matter, they will dim the faculties developed unnaturally through certain chemicals or plants independently of the spiritual world. Apprentices who gain a certain forced clairvoyance without having first acquired purity, virtue, self-control, run the risk of finishing very badly.

To develop clairvoyance you must have a reverent attitude and not try to bluff the powers of purity and light. You must be prepared, you must ask for permission from the divine beings before entering their regions even to admire their beauty and purity and to glorify God. In that way you gain their friendship and you will not be opposed or rejected.

Unfortunately in this epoch children are taught to be rude and bold, to have no respect, to be superficial and violent. That is the way an adult must behave supposedly, in order to succeed in life; any show of kindness or honesty would entail poverty and misery! Children are told, 'You have to cheat and lie to succeed in life, do what you must and don't be stupid.' I grant you that crude and wicked people exist in the world who deserve to be given a lesson or two, but why have that attitude toward creatures who are our superiors? Why not try to win their friendship and trust by showing them respect, even reverence, instead of trying to impose our wills and violence on them also.

For instance, try and tell scientists that the scientific attitude toward animals is criminal, you will be considered an imbecile. They are convinced that in the name of science, for the sake of scientific advancement, they can experiment on animals and slaughter them at will. That they have not worked to develop any more subtle, intellectual faculties is shown by the fact that they do their research on live creatures and are not averse to killing them by the thousands. If they were spiritual, they would find other and better ways of healing mankind. But Nature has decided to give them a good lesson in the not too distant future.

It cannot be denied that our century far surpasses other centuries as far as intellectual prowess and technical knowledge are concerned, but it is also the most decadent century. Nothing is sacred to humans, they are violent, vulgar and superficial. And now I come along to tell you the great truths (no one else takes the trouble), one of them being that purity and reverence awaken faculties within you that will let you see reality. At first you will perceive inwardly with your mind, for the inner eye affects primarily the highest regions of your being, and then you will begin to see objectively in the invisible world, just as you see objects in the physical world. Only purity opens the way for this new vision.

My interpretation of the words, *'If thine eye be single thy whole body will be in the light,'* is that it is not the two physical eyes but the third, inner eye, that must be pure. It is not so for instance, that the pureness of the body depends on the eye, especially not on one eye: both eyes depend on the purity of the blood on the body, if the bloodstream is contaminated, the eyes will be also because they are part of the body. The third eye does not belong to the physical body, it is above it. Without the esoteric Science, the words of Jesus are unintelligible, meaningless.

Hence purity... you see I always come back to purity... is a quality above all others that man must not avoid but on the contrary work all his life to gain, all his life he should work to understand purity and love purity and try to become pure in all his actions. Without purity he will not advance, and should he insist on trying to acquire psychic powers without purity, the spirits of the invisible world will not tolerate this violation, and will take their revenge.

If you manage to awaken your third eye without first developing love, kindness, indulgence, self-control, you will see what lies in wait for you! You will suddenly be able to see the vices and crimes hidden deep inside others, you will be forced to see the evil entities, monsters and larvae that attach themselves to your friends and, unable to bear what you see, you will entreat God night and day to take away your gift of clairvoyance. You will remember with regret the time when you could see nothing, for illusion is in this case a thousand times better than clairvoyance.

But if you have conquered a number of your weaknesses, if you have prepared yourself and are purified, if you have gained control and learned to love humans, then you will no longer see only the horrors, you will see what corresponds to your level of consciousness, and... you will be able to contemplate the glorious future of mankind. Even though certain things may disturb and distress you, with the love, courage and self-discipline you now have you will not succumb to despair, you will be above fear and even be able to assist by contributing helpful thoughts.

Clairvoyance is awarded to each one according to his degree of evolution. If you are still on the lower levels, the Hell you see will cause you great suffering. If you want to see the glory of God and the Heavenly Hosts, you must be evolved, pure and enlightened. Then if you wish to go down into Hell and study and investigate it, you can. A man or woman with the gift of clairvoyance does not necessarily see everything, there are different degrees of clairvoyance that correspond with the degree of purity in the clairvoyant: the purer he is, the better he will be able to see in the celestial regions, but he will see nothing but crawling beasts, devouring monsters and wild animals on the prowl if he has not purified himself. You should not attempt to become clairvoyant without preparation.

There is no need for hurry to become clairvoyant, it is not really desirable and in the end leads only to grief and disgust at having to live amongst humans. Nor is it desirable to have too keen a sense of smell. Fortunately man's sense of smell is still rudimentary because otherwise no one would be able to stand the odour caused by our defective way of eating, living and thinking. Observe yourself: when you give way to anger, jealousy or hatred, your body emanates a most unpleasant odour; when you are in a state of intense spirituality, you emanate a pleasant subtle odour, proving that our thoughts, feelings and intentions affect our glands and secretions with resulting pleasant or repulsive exhalations.

People who eat a lot of meat and smoke and drink alcohol generally emanate an unpleasant odour; the poison they eat and drink exudes from their pores... how can they stand each other, even sharing a bed together for years? And on the beaches in summer, when people are piled on top of each other for miles... if you are at all sensitive, you can smell from a distance the miasmas and nauseating clouds hovering over them. Fortunately most people are not terribly sensitive, if they were they would have a permanent need to vomit, and would not know where to turn to get away from each other.

The same is true for the inner eye. As long as you are not capable of dominating disgust or fear, you must not awaken the inner eye. The disciple must conquer fear and repugnance before venturing to confront the terrifying creatures in the lower world, expecting them to obey his commands.

You no doubt have read the novel by Bulwer-Lytton, 'Zanoni,' in which the hero, Glyndon, disobeys his Master, Mejnour, and inhales the Elixir of Eternal Life. Because he is not prepared, the Guardian of the Hearth is what he summons, and he loses consciousness. He is pursued and tormented by the monster until finally Zanoni delivers him. I have told you before what the Guardian of the Hearth represents, the terrible image that everyone must face one day. If you have not been prepared, if you lack strength, self-control, courage, force, and especially purity, to keep you calm and unperturbed, what will happen? The Guardian of the Hearth can do nothing against purity and audacity, one order, 'Begone!' is enough to make the monster vanish. He is afraid of purity and light. But he is terrifying with cowards and weaklings. Like dogs in the street, if you run from them they run after you and bite your ankles, but if you turn and stare at them, they flee.

The Guardian of the Hearth is the same: purity alone gives the assurance and courage you must have when you confront him. A man who knows that his life is pure is upheld by that knowledge and is never afraid; it is only when he has broken the law or committed a crime that he becomes fearful. When

Adam and Eve had eaten the forbidden fruit, they knew fear and hid themselves. A creature that breaks the law, even if no one has seen him, becomes guilty and fearful, he loses his daring, his walk and gestures betray his lack of confidence, his ideas become confused, he hesitates and stammers.

To get back to clairvoyance, I would like to add a few more words.

As I explained, the lower region of the Moon is a region of mist and fog, that is, of illusion, of mental aberration: this is the region of *Yesod* that most mediums, healers, radiesthesists, clairvoyants, are in touch with. I am not saying they are not true mediums and clairvoyants, but what I have against them is their pretentiousness. A fellow who thinks he has a gift of healing or mediumnity is not above sending messages to an Initiate or a great Master for instance, offering to instruct him by divulging messages, and what messages! It would be better if he instructed himself before trying to instruct others! It is easy to commit errors, to be wrong, unless you have thoroughly studied and investigated this science in which the official science also plays a part. It is incredible what some people relate! Mediums have given me messages purported to have come directly from God (whom I have never doubted, I would not so offend Him), but since it was He who distributed intelligence and logic and reason in the first place, I use these gifts of His to think, to reason with, and I see that these particular messages are in direct contradiction to what He has already told me. You see how odd this business is!

You say, 'But how do you dare to criticize messages and directives that come from God?' I do not criticize them, but I cannot help seeing how illogical and contradictory the messages are. It may be that they come from God, but let us say rather that they come from several gods, the astral plane is full of entities longing to play the role of God, and we who are without discernment fall into their trap. The world is swarming with people who think they can instruct others, predict their future and so on... and the information always comes straight from the mouth of God! If it were really God speaking through the intervention of these people, the messages would at least all have the same style and content, the same divine Wisdom... whereas in some of the messages God says things that are grandiose and sublime, and in others the advice is puerile and senseless.

One day I was reproached by God (through the intermediary of one of these clairvoyants) for not praying to Him, for never asking Him for help. I who have done nothing else all my life... I was astounded! Has God not listened to a whole lifetime of prayer? How surprising, yes, unbelievably surprising! Besides which, it seems He advises me to cut my bonds with the Masters and Initiates of the past because if not, my work will be impeded. How can I believe that God would urge me to turn my back on wonderful beings who worked for Him all their lives, magnificent examples such as Buddha, Zoroaster, Moses, Jesus? Look at the silly advice that can be given in the name of the Lord! This is serious, dear brothers and sisters, serious and dangerous.

I advise prophets, mediums, messengers from Heaven, to learn how to receive messages with greater discernment before giving me or anyone else their messages, to verify where they come from and be a little less blind and gullible. They will learn that there are entities in the invisible world who love to play pranks on humans... how many people have been fooled by highly intelligent and malicious spirits! Unless you are more intelligent and knowing than they, you are lost.[5]

How many women come to see me in the middle of the night announcing they are there by invitation: my voice told them to come! So convinced are they that I am not able to convince them it is not so! My voice told them to come just like that in the middle of the night, to create a child with me. The voice apparently also told them to come knocking on my door and wake me up without any respect or consideration! I try to send them away by saying that I too hear voices telling me that their voice was false and misleading, that they are victims of their own wild imaginings, but they continue to believe in their voices in spite of all the proofs to the contrary! Finally, there is nothing to do but eject them. Do you see how hard it is to make humans see the truth?

Another prevalent habit of the brothers and sisters is to give very precise details on your prior incarnations. If you believed, I wonder what would become of you! It is never bad things, it is all wonderful, you were always a king or queen, a pharaoh, St. Anthony, St. Francis of Assisi, St. Theresa of the Holy Child or whatever, and so and so was your wife or husband. They have ideas as to who my wife and daughter were in the past also... how is it that I feel absolutely no affinity with my former wife or daughter? Have I forgotten everything? I wonder why it is I don't seem to recognize my own! I may have affinities, but never apparently with those who have been my wife or daughter!

I am not saying never to believe in those things, no, there is often a smattering of truth in them. A being who has become sensitized, psychically developed, may capture messages from the invisible world, but it is extremely rare that someone becomes perfected in this area and we should realize that what someone who thinks he is clairvoyant perceives may not be true. People may have mediumistic faculties, they may be extremely perceptive, but what they tell you may be a mixture of truth and falsehood... you should always verify. In any case none of that is really useful. What good is it to reveal the past of the brothers and sisters? If it were really desirable I would be the first to do it: I do not. You may think it is because I lack the faculties that others possess... think what you will.

I repeat, it is neither psychologically nor pedagogically wise to talk to humans about their past incarnations. There will come the time when you will be able to do it yourself, but first you must have complete control. If you knew that someone had been your great enemy in the past, that he had assassinated you, what would happen unless you are very strong, very much in control of yourself? This kind of revelation is dangerous, it can affect your evolution. If it were so important for humans to know the past, why would Providence hide it from them? If Providence chooses to make them forget, there must be a reason. Maybe it is to protect them.

When you have no idea that someone has wronged you in a past incarnation, you like him, you even help him, but if you knew, what would you do? If a father and mother bring children into the world and care for them lovingly without any idea that they were enemies in a past life, their devotion erases the Karma they have incurred. If they had known, what might they not have done, including abandoning the children! Providence leaves parents in ignorance so that they can carry out their responsibility as well as possible. Rare are those who can receive this kind of revelation without danger, they must be very evolved, very controlled.

How many things to say on this subject! People who have an interest in your money, in taking advantage of you, will invent magnificent incarnations for your past so that you will be taken in and go along with their wishes. If you really wanted to help people you would reveal their mistakes, their shortcomings, rather than making them think they were kings, geniuses or saints, especially when it is not true. I know that people do not like to be told of their shortcomings but if you have the courage to do it regardless, it proves that you seek nothing for yourself, but are completely disinterested. When you tell a friend something unpleasant to help him avoid disaster, even at the risk of losing his friendship, then you are truly his friend, a real friend. If he becomes angry and avoids you, it is just as well it happened... what can you do with a friend who only wants compliments and praise? Try him out by saying something negative and, depending upon his reaction, his comprehension, you will know what to reveal to him about the past or the future.[6]

Dear brothers and sisters, remember that many clairvoyants are still limited to the obscure, hazy regions of *Yesod*, they have not gone higher and cannot lay hands on anything but a few reflections of the invisible world that will do nothing but lead you astray. Clarity, crystal clear limpidity, exists only in the higher regions of *Yesod* where the Angels live, the Bearers of Life, pure Life that opens the eyes. Those who can rise into that clarity, yes, those are the ones of whom it is said that they shall see God.

The Bonfin, 5th September, 1966

Notes

1. See *Sons and Daughters of God,* Izvor Coll. n° 240, chap. 7: '.The Man Jesus, and the cosmic principle of the Christ'.
2. See *The Philosopher's Stone – in the Gospels and in Alchemy,* Izvor Coll. n° 241, chap. I-2: 'The word of God'.
3. See *The Faith That Moves Mountains,* Izvor Coll. n° 238, chap. 10: 'Identifying with God'.
4. See *Looking into the Invisible – Intuition, Clairvoyance, Dreams,* Izvor Coll. n° 228, chap. 10: 'The Spiritual Eye'.
5. Op. cit., chap. 5: 'Should We Consult Clairvoyants?'.
6. See *What is a Spiritual Master?,* Izvor Coll. n° 207, chap. 6: 'A Master is a Mirror Reflecting the Truth'.

Chapter Eleven

THE GATES OF THE NEW JERUSALEM

You have had to listen to a great deal of talk about purity these last few days, dear brothers and sisters, but it was necessary because of the many aspects of purity. Religions have presented purity under the aspect of chastity mainly, and it is true, chastity is a part of purity, but a minor part.

Today if you like, I will talk about the twelve doors of the Holy City, New Jerusalem.

It says in the *Book of Revelation, 'And I John saw... the holy city, New Jerusalem, descending out of Heaven from God, having the glory of God and her light was like unto a stone most precious, even like a jasper stone, clear as crystal; and had a great wall great and high, and had twelve gates, and at the gates twelve angels and names written thereon, which are the names of the twelve tribes of the children of Israel; on the east three gates, on the north three gates, on the south three gates and on the west three gates... and the twelve gates were twelve pearls, every several gate was of one pearl, and the street of the city was pure gold, as it were transparent glass.'*

You say, 'Each gate a single pearl... but that would take giant oysters! Do they have giant oysters up there?' A pearl is a symbol. In the esoteric science a pearl symbolizes purity, and is consecrated to the Moon because of that purity.

A gate is to permit people to go from one place to another, if not human beings then currents, forces, or entities. The question of gates is fundamental. The *Book of Revelation* talks about the twelve gates of the Heavenly Jerusalem, the Kabala talks about the fifty gates of *Binah*... what about a child being born on earth, does he not pass through a gate? The human being also has gates or doors, not only physical doors, but spiritual ones, which are often closed: purity consists in opening these doors to the celestial beings... which may appear obtuse for the moment, but be patient....

I have talked to you before on the subject of New Jerusalem, and you are not among those waiting for it to come down out of the heavens![1] People have been waiting for two thousand years... they can wait another thousand years, it will not come that way. New Jerusalem is a symbol. When you talk about a city, you include the citizens also; the Jerusalem described as descending from Heaven represents a whole category of creatures so pure and so highly evolved that each one has twelve doors open at all times to the divine currents.

What are the two eyes? Two doors. What are the two ears? Two doors. And the two nasal passages? Two more doors through which pass the currents, Ida and Pingala.[2] Six doors to which we will add the mouth, which makes seven doors. There are two more on the breast which, although they do not function at the moment in men, are nevertheless doors. The tenth door is the navel, and the umbilical cord is the door through which the mother feeds her child with her blood and all the other elements he needs before birth. I leave it to you to discover the last two doors, bringing the total to twelve. Is it not extraordinary to see how Nature has formed the human body so that everyone has twelve doors? But the doors do not function well most of the time, they are obstructed and there is no way to open them: the eyes see, but imperfectly because they are too often trained on things that are negative and ugly; the ears hear, but in the wrong way, or else they retain only what is flattering (or vexing) to the personality; the mouth opens, but often to pronounce harmful, destructive or meaningless words.

When St. John described the Heavenly Jerusalem as a city made of gold, precious stones and a light that never dimmed, he meant that in time there will come down from Heaven highly evolved and pure beings who will shine with inner light, the sons and daughters of God bringing the new Teaching.

There is much more to say about doors. You are surprised sometimes because I insist on the need to keep the doors of a house closed, yes, it surprises you to see that I dwell on such insignificant details. But accidents and tragedy come from not knowing when to close doors and when to open them, what to close and what to open. If it were a question of physical doors it would not be so important, but there are other doors and those are the ones I am talking about. Behind the physical world there is another world, and when I see that brothers and sisters have an unconscious habit of leaving their doors open, I know that their inner doors are also wide open for the undesirables to enter at will. They will not be able to hold on to the spiritual riches they are given, and as everything is wide open, they will be robbed.[3]

People complain to me when they go home after a stay at Izgrev or the Bonfin that they lose their enthusiasm and zest. The reason is simple: they were not able to hold on to the light and spiritual warmth they received while they were here. You ask, 'How can we hold on to those things?' By keeping the doors closed. If our inspiration vanishes so quickly, it is because in our ignorance we leave the doors open and thieves enter and take it all away. There are many things to think about that never occur to us. When there is too much noise next door or in an adjoining room, you go and close the door and shut out the noise. You do that on the physical plane but you leave everything wide open on the astral plane and then you wonder why you are ill or disturbed. It is far-reaching, this question of doors. Your heart and your mind are also doors, but as you do not know when they should be open and when they should be shut, you let in the thieves and leave God outside.

Our entire life is based on these two operations, closing and opening. Shells and oysters teach us that lesson, but we have not grasped it. The shells opening and closing teach us that life is a question of a constant opening and closing of doors. Man must learn when to open the door and when to keep it closed, for unless he does he will never be pure.

As for the pearl, there are many things to say about it. How does an oyster create the pearl? The pearl starts out as a tiny grain of sand in the shell, an irritant, a difficulty for the oyster. 'Ah,' he says to himself. 'How am I going to get rid of this sand? It scratches, it irritates me, but I have no arms or legs to hit it with. What am I going to do?' This makes the oyster think. It concentrates, it meditates, it seeks advice, and it finds out that there is a chemical process of transformation, if you take elements and combine them with the right influences according to the phases of the Moon. That is something you did not know. And so the oyster goes to work. Of course it takes a long time to make a pearl because an oyster has active periods and inactive ones. How do I know all this? By observation.

Oysters secrete a special substance in which they envelop the grain of sand when it is rough and rasping until it becomes smooth, polished, velvety. And when it works the oysters are happy and say to themselves, 'Ah, I have overcome a difficulty!' For thousands of years humans could have been learning from pearl oysters, but they are too shortsighted to see that there is a lesson to be learned. What lesson? That they should do the same. Why not take your difficulties and everything that worries or irritates you and wrap them in a luminous rainbow of light? You would be developing tremendous riches within. The disciples must understand that they should work on their problems and transform them into precious pearls, which may seem like a story from the Arabian Nights, but it is true. Real disciples wrap their problems and even their enemies in light, and use them to become rich and strong. As long as you do nothing but complain, as long as you are unhappy and miserable, you will not be able to secrete this special substance in which to wrap your difficulties.

If I told you how many pearls I possess thanks to all the difficulties I have encountered in my life! When someone comes here who is unbearable, I rejoice, I say to myself, 'Lord God, what luck! Another prospective pearl!' And I give you all an extraordinary conference without your knowing that the subject is there in the Hall, a little grain of sand that disturbs me and becomes my inspiration, the reason I can give a good lecture! I do not pretend to have transformed all my problems into precious pearls (I would not make such a pronouncement even if it were so, in order not to provoke the invisible world), but just the same, there have been a good many grains of sand that I have enveloped. And you, what do you do when you are faced with a difficulty? Do you use it as a means to go higher, to reinforce yourselves? I doubt it. Get going! How much longer will I be around to talk to you of these things? If you understand the image of the pearl oyster, you will have enough work for the rest of your life.

You have read in the Gospels the parable of the man who, when he found the pearl of great price he was seeking, went and sold all his possessions in order to be able to purchase the pearl. You have to understand what the pearl of great price is and why this man sold everything to have it. It is symbolic.

The white of a pearl is indicative, its emanations relate it to the Moon. On the Sephirotic Tree, the pearl oyster is *Yesod* the foundation, the base which corresponds symbolically with the genital organs where the pearl is formed. The pearl represents the quintessence of pure, disinterested love, the feminine principle, the woman who brings into the world a pearl, the child. Like oysters that cannot form a pure and shining, perfect pearl (like the black ones I brought back from Japan) sometimes women give birth to a child who will grow up to be a criminal. The pearl is the child.

As a symbol a pearl has many interpretations. The pearl oyster, the feminine principle, forms the Christ Child within us, that is, the body of glory. We are oysters who must form the precious pearl, the body of glory, the body of immortality, the body of light, the body of Christ, with our quintessence.[4]

I have already explained what St. John meant by this extraordinary image of the New Jerusalem descending from Heaven with its twelve gates of pearl. Let us come back to purity for I have not finished with the depth and richness of purity.

To take the question of virginity and chastity: many people imagine that purity is no more than physical chastity, and look upon all physical contact as impure. But there were many sages and prophets who were married, and even if not married themselves, they were born of a mother and father, and what did this father and mother have in order to bring them into the world? Physical contact! And what made it possible for them to bring Initiates, Masters, Prophets, Divinities, into the world? They were pure. When the physical contact between humans is gross and sensual, then yes, they are impure, but when the contact is sublimated by an ideal, a pure love, and accomplished according to divine methods, then they open the door for divinities to come on earth.[5]

When great Masters incarnate on earth, there must always be a man and a woman who make it possible for them to be born. In their union there is nothing sensual or passionate, the physical body is but a means, an instrument that serves because it is impossible to do otherwise. Behind the physical contact are divine, luminous impulses, and then it is geniuses and divinities that incarnate. Krishna, Jesus – Christians know nothing about the birth of Jesus – were born in that way.

No creature has ever arrived on the physical plane without a mother and father being responsible (I am not going to discuss artificial insemination at this time). Perhaps in a very distant future it will be possible, I have given several lectures on the fact that one day children will not be born as they are now. But until then humans will go on with joy or with disgust, who knows, having physical contacts in order to perpetuate the human race. There will always be a few altruists to keep from letting the human race die out, and it will not be a few mystics and puritans with their bizarre theories that will stop them!

I am sorry if I shock some of you, but I have done research and compared beliefs with Nature and I find that the tales of virgin births through the operation of the Holy Spirit are in complete contradiction with everything that goes on in Nature. Whether you accept this or not is all the same to me, I tell you the truth... if you do not accept it, then it will be for those who come later.

A man and woman conceive a child in utmost purity if there is no passion or desire involved. But to say that it is the Holy Spirit who fathers a child, no. If it were really the Holy Spirit why is the child not born immediately without spending nine months in a woman's womb? To be conceived by the Holy Spirit is possible, but not as is generally supposed. The Holy Spirit implies forces, faculties, and feelings that are absolutely pure, that contain nothing human or earthly. Anyone who is inhabited by the Holy Spirit can bring a divine child into the world, that is how nearly all the great founders of religions came into the world, including Jesus. But Christians are unable to accept that. The birth of Jesus was presented as stories are presented to children who are not old enough to hear the truth, and now nothing can shake their belief! It is not up to me to convince them of the opposite, let them hold on to their beliefs if it helps them.[6]

Now, I ask you to keep inside you the image of New Jerusalem descending from Heaven. Think of yourself as being in this celestial city with the twelve gates made of a single pearl, that is, with eyes that see, with ears that hear, with a mouth that utters magic words to aid, enlighten and vivify mankind. I will not yet reveal the five other functions of each door. At the moment you know of two, but you have no idea what to do with these doors. Let us leave all that aside, these things are too profound, too sacred. They are the Holy Mysteries, pearls that the invisible world forbids me to reveal to everyone. One day maybe, but to receive these revelations, you need to work a lot more!

Be patient, I will give you more explanations on purity, for great are the Mysteries of *Yesod*.

The Bonfin, 7th September, 1966

Notes

1. See *A New Dawn – Society and Politics in the Light of Initiatic Science,* Complete Works, vol. 26, chap. 6: 'The New Jerusalem'.
2. See *Light is a Living Spirit,* Izvor Coll. n° 212, chap. 9: 'The Spiritual Laser', Part I.
3. See *The Tree of the Knowledge of Good and Evil,* Izvor Coll. n° 210, chap. 7: 'The Undesirables'.
4. See *'You Are Gods',* Synopsis Coll., Part IX, chap. 4: 'The body of glory'.
5. See *'Cherchez le Royaume de Dieu et sa Justice',* Synopsis Coll., Part VIII, chap. 2: 'Faire descendre des divinités sur la terre'.
6. See *Noël et le mystère de la naissance du Christ,* Brochure n° 321.

Part III

LOVE AND SEX

Question: Master, would you talk to us about the distinction between love and sexuality, and whether sexuality has any place in the spiritual life?

This is a good question: it concerns everyone for it is the most important thing in life. You can discuss all kinds of things, mathematics, astronomy, chemistry, physics, but you will interest only a few that way... whereas the subject of love, show me anyone who is not interested! Yes, young or old. I am not sure how qualified I am to answer your questions, but I have one advantage, I see things from a point of view that is very, very significant. My life has been consecrated to obtaining this particular point of view.

Before I begin, I will say a word to explain this, so that you who are here for the first time will not be in such a hurry to criticize and think to yourselves, 'Oh, my! There are books and books on love and sex that have much more to say than he has... what an ignoramus!' I admit to being ignorant, why not? Nevertheless the authors of those books lack something I have, which is my particular point of view! Nor do they understand the subject in quite the same way. I leave it to you to go to doctors and psychiatrists, etc., and read their books, but I will give you something else; a point of view that is virtually non-existent elsewhere.

What is this point of view? Here is an example: a professor with degrees from several universities is working in his laboratory on his formulas, whilst his twelve year old son is in the garden climbing trees. All at once the child calls out to his father, 'I see my aunt and uncle walking on the road!' The father asks the child for information, 'How far away are they? Are they carrying anything?' And the child informs the father. With all his knowledge the father cannot see as far as his young and ignorant son, because the child has climbed up to a place that allows him to see far and wide whilst the father is below within the four walls of his laboratory.

This image is to make you see that useful as it may be to have learning and faculties, your point of view is also most important. I have always sought the highest point of view. As I have said, I am neither intelligent nor learned (I am the ignorant twelve year old), but I have been made to climb to the heights and I see things from there that even the greatest scholars and scientists do not see. I admit to being mediocre, but I have a point of view that allows me to see things differently.[1]

To observe the universe from the level of the ground is not the same as observing it from the sun. You say, 'But the sun comes up and the sun goes down, the stars rise and set...' True, but also not true! It is true if you are standing on the earth, gazing at them from the geocentric point of view, but it is not true if you observe them from the heliocentric point of view. People observe everything from the world's point of view and say, 'You must eat, you must earn money, you must sleep with women...' but if they observed things from the solar level, the divine, spiritual point of view, they would see things differently. That is my point of view, and that is what permits me to show you love and sexuality in another light.

At first glance, it is hard to separate the two. On a physical plane they are easy to confound. Sexuality, the natural instinct that urges humans and animals to reproduce themselves, is fostered by Nature to keep the species from disappearing. There is no love in sexuality. Love is a force that comes from above, whereas sexuality... although an energy that comes originally from above (it is even a divine energy), in the human being it is influenced by the way he thinks and feels, and, if he behaves like an animal, the energy no longer manifests itself as divine energy.

Everything comes from God and everything that manifests itself through man as energy is originally divine energy,[2] but this energy has different effects depending upon the conductor, the person through whom it manifests. Like electricity... electricity is an energy (we are still in the dark as to its nature) that changes depending upon where it is. When it is passing through a lamp it becomes light, yet electricity is not light; when it passes through a radiator it becomes heat, when passing through a magnet it becomes magnetism, when passing through a ventilator it becomes movement. In the same way cosmic force assumes a certain aspect depending upon which one of the human organs it is passing through: in the brain it becomes intelligence, the capacity to reason; in the solar plexus or the Hara centre, it becomes feeling or sentiment; in the muscular system it becomes movement; and finally, when it passes through the sexual organs, it becomes attraction for the opposite sex. The energy transforms itself according to the region it is in.

The energy itself comes from above but when it traverses the sexual organs it awakens sensuous desires, manifestations in which there is no love. At certain periods of the year, animals couple, but is love involved? They tear each other apart, or as in the case of certain insects like spiders or the praying mantis, the female devours the male... is that love? No, it is sexuality. It begins to be love when the energy reaches other centres such as the heart, the brain, the soul and spirit; there is still a desire to be near someone but the attraction is illuminated by thoughts, ideas, a sense of the aesthetic, which lift it above the mere selfish craving for satisfaction regardless of the other person.

Love is sexuality if you wish, but an enlarged, enlightened, transformed sexuality. The degrees and manifestations of love are too numerous to mention or classify. For instance, a man can love a pretty woman without being physically attracted to her, all he wants is her happiness, health, and wealth in every way. What do you call that? It is love, not sexuality and is therefore on a higher level... still, isn't there a little bit of sexuality in this love, for otherwise why was the young man not drawn to someone else, a plainer, older woman, a man friend? Yes, in most cases you will find at least a little sexual attraction.

Sexuality also has degrees. When the higher degrees of the cosmic force enter you, they bring you into the heavenly regions where you are not limited to physical sensations as are people who, once their desire is satisfied, separate and even begin to fight! All they ask for is to be relieved, calmed and appeased; in time, when the energy accumulates, they will be smiling and tender with each other again. These are calculated, premeditated tricks that man uses in order to satisfy his animal appetites.

But love is not to be confused with sex. It is normal especially for the young to have needs and desires, Nature has foreseen what is necessary for the propagation of the race; if men and women had no impulses or instincts humanity would come to an end. Nature urges creatures to come together physically, but love is something other than that.

How many brothers and sisters come to ask me if they can get married! I ask questions to be sure they have a clear idea of what they are getting into, 'How do you love each other, is it entirely a physical attraction, or do you also love each other's sensitivity, the way you feel about things? Do you also have an intellectual attraction, do you appreciate each other's way of thinking and seeing things? For your marriage to work out, you must be in harmony with each other on three levels, and each level has its own particularities.'

Physical attraction alone cannot last. It does not take long to become sated and disgusted if that is all that attracts you to one another. The other two bonds, those of thoughts and feelings are more stable and permanent. If you disagree with each other's thoughts and feelings, you may be dying for each other physically but in no time you will be fighting. When your sensuality has been appeased, your longing satisfied through having seen and tasted everything, then the differences surface, the oppositions become apparent, the fighting begins: the differences make you want to kill each other.

Therefore think about these things... young people usually do not. A boy and girl who are drawn to each other physically never look to see whether they get along on the other levels, all that is most important is put aside. Later, the chasm between the two grows wider and wider, the upsetting arguments come more and more frequently, and in the end it finishes very badly. How many times have I seen this! Sometimes it is the opposite that happens, people who feel no physical attraction for each other and don't even like each other, discover that they have the same ideas in common, the same likes and dislikes, the same philosophy... it is wonderful! They start by seeing each other, then they begin to admire each other, and finally they love each other so much that they fall in love physically as well! Mutual ideas and feelings are essential to a good marriage, that is what young boys and girls must realize; if not, they will separate in a very short time. To fall in love is not enough, there must be an understanding on the three levels: physical, emotional and intellectual.[3]

Take the traditional marriage amongst the Turks and other Eastern peoples in the past: young people were made to marry without laying eyes on each other before the day of the ceremony, their marriage was arranged by their parents or perhaps by the reigning sovereign. And so of course there were surprises... a girl might find herself married to a hunchback, a cripple, a blindman! And often in spite of all that, although the first days were unbearable, as time went by the young couple discovered more and more things to like and admire in each other until they actually fell in love! That is the extraordinary thing! Now they choose each other in spite of all the warning signals, all opposition parental or otherwise, and then separate in a short time even though they did the choosing themselves! How do you explain this phenomenon? It is not just a question of sexuality or eroticism as sexologists will tell you... experts who don't even know why homosexuality is rampant in the world once again. Remember before you marry, to study the person from all angles to see whether you will get along in the emotional, philosophic, aesthetic realms as well as in the physical. Otherwise you are courting trouble.

To come back to your question on the subject of love and sexuality, I will say that sexuality is a purely selfish longing on the part of someone seeking pleasure, his own pleasure whereas love, real love, is based on sacrifice, the sacrifice of your time, your efforts, your money, in order to permit the other person to blossom out and develop to his full capacity. Nothing is more beautiful than love, the kind of love that makes you want to give something of yourself, to deprive yourself in order to give to someone else. Like a mother, her love for her child has nothing to do with sensuality. During wars, what privation mothers go through for their children, they die of starvation to feed the child. That is love!

Spirituality begins when love triumphs over sexuality, when a human being is able to give up something inside himself for the good of the other. If you are unable to deprive yourself of anything whatsoever, it is not love. When a man throws himself on a girl to satisfy himself, does he think about the harm he may be doing her? No, he is ready to kill her to satisfy himself. That is sexuality, the animal instinct. You say, 'But there is nothing divine in that!' Sexuality has divine origins, but if humans cannot control themselves, the way they express love will not be divine. The good thing about sexuality is that it is effective in reproducing the species, but when it is purely for pleasure, it is a waste. Unbelievable things have been invented in the name of pleasure, the pill of course, and all kinds of other inventions that I do not wish even to mention, that are for enjoyment only and have nothing to do with propagating the race.

I do not wish to discuss whether these things should exist or not. At this stage of mankind's development, moralists and even the religious accept the situation because they know that man's lower, animal nature is still so primitive, so strong that if it were not allowed to manifest itself, it would make matters worse. I will not discuss it now, but it is sad to think that man is so low that he cannot control his energy and put it to use for a divine purpose, for spiritual work, instead of stimulating it for the sake of wallowing in pleasure. It would take too long now but one day I will tell you the bad ramifications of this, not the least being that man is held back on the inferior plane and grows stupider and more brutish until he has lost all his psychic possibilities. On the other hand it does maintain a certain balance.

Actually the question is very complicated especially if one is married and no longer free. If you continue to act as if you were free, the result will be trouble. A wife whose husband is built like a bull, even if her nature is spiritual, has to give in to him, otherwise he will resort to violence, or infidelity. You see how many anomalies there can be in a marriage between two people, who are ill assorted. When a bull marries a dove, what can there be but trouble?

But do not conclude from this that I am against marriage. I say only that it is a dangerous, hazardous undertaking, the outcome of which is unknown. Marriage is a coming together of two strangers, two unknown factors and the result is also unknown. At first each one displays himself to his best advantage, but later on, their weaknesses, their sickness, their mental or physical cruelty become apparent. It is a risk...

Sexuality is love, but love that has for goal the satisfaction of the self. From the external point of view, there is no difference between love and sexuality... always the same gestures, the same embraces, the same kisses. The difference is in the direction the energies take. When you are sensual you pay very little attention to the other person, whereas when you love, you think above all about making the other person happy. Love and sexuality are the same on the physical plane but on the invisible plane, the psychic, spiritual plane, they are very different. In what way? That is what I am about to tell you.

None of the physiologists, psychiatrists, sexologists, have discovered what happens during the sexual act on the more subtle planes, the etheric, fluidic plane. They know about tension, excitement, ejection, all that is carefully studied and classified today. What they do not know is that in the first case, that of a purely physical, biological, egoistic sexuality, the volcanic eruptions that take place manifest as ugly forms, coarse emanations, thick and muddy colours with a dirty dark red predominating, and these emanations go down into the earth where creatures wait in the shadows to feast on this vital energy. Yes, lovers provide a feast for dark creatures with low appetites.

In the past on the occasion of a marriage or a great victory over the enemy, the kings and princes celebrated by ordering public feasts that lasted several days, sometimes a week, and all the beggars, the homeless and disinherited came to the feast because there was something there for them. You see, it is the same thing, but science has not yet explored this aspect of sexuality. When a man and woman are making exchanges, they are holding a feast, a public festival attended by creatures of all kinds. Even under conditions of utmost secrecy, there are always these visitors who come to the feast, and more often than not they are the ones to absorb everything, because in all this effusiveness there is nothing or at least very little for the soul, the spirit and the divine side. That is why exchanges between lovers are seldom of benefit to them, but rather the opposite. After a while they change, they lose something, their looks, their colour, the way they move... their whole way of being changes, the life and light they had before is no longer there. All because the love they felt was inferior and they let in the dark creatures instead of inviting the Angels and Archangels and all the luminous spirits, who they too, love to feast.

When a magus is beginning a ceremony involving the invisible world, he traces a circle around himself for protection. Outside that circle he can be threatened with injury and harm, thunder and lightning and everything else, but they cannot enter, inside the circle he is as safe as in a fortress.[4] Humans are not aware of this important fact, no one has taught them how to protect themselves in any way, which led me one day to say something rather daring: it is the way human beings love each other that is at the base of all the evil in the world: wars, disease, unhappiness exist in the world because there are people who make love like animals in a blind, stupid, careless, disgusting, diabolical way, this is what furnishes the evil spirits with material to use against humanity, it strengthens and feeds the spirits who are there for the purpose of doing harm to mankind. If men and women knew this, they would be so sad, so unhappy and heartsick that they would try to love each other in some other way that would bring the Kingdom of God and His Right-eousness on earth. They would understand that only the spiritualisation of love will bring in the Kingdom of God. That is why the question of love is so important.

The state of humanity at the moment is the result of the fact that love is not used for a divine, glorious goal but for pleasure, pleasure that has an ill effect on men. You say, 'But then do you mean that pleasure should be suppressed entirely?' No, if you learn how to love, you will have ten times more pleasure, for real pleasure is the result of an act that is in harmony with other substances, other presences. When it is in perfect harmony with the divine world, pleasure is multiplied and increased to infinity. Pleasure as you know it is so gross, so inferior, so costly it is hardly worth it. Pleasure is necessary, but why not a pleasure so subtle that it reveals the whole universe to you, that it makes you luminous and beautiful, expressive and powerful and strong and useful? That pleasure is worthwhile indeed, and Nature will never deprive you of it.

This is the truth of the matter, dear brothers and sisters, and believe me I am inventing nothing. Love is the greatest mystery in existence. No one really knows what it is, everyone goes on practicing what they mistakenly think is love. That is why everyone is still groping around miserably, with no change in sight. No matter how many more extraordinary discoveries science makes, as long as the question of love remains unclear in human minds, mankind will never get out of its difficulties. That is the point of view I have been given.

How should one love? You will learn from the Teaching. There is no one who does not eat, but no one eats correctly; no one who does not work, but no one works correctly; no one who does not breathe, but no one breathes correctly; no one who does not love but no one loves correctly. We all think we know how to eat, breathe, think, etc. No, and we don't know how to work either. 'What do you mean, we don't know how to work?' No, when you work you are tense, resentful, grudging, and that makes you ill. Everyone thinks that work is tiring: I say it is not work but the way in which you work that makes you ill and tired. Work brings health, happiness and joy! Without work one is lost.[5]

A few days ago I talked to you about the way in which you should handle objects, how to pick up your glass, how to pour water as if your whole body was singing and dancing. Try handling objects with love: you will see that the harmony of your gestures reflects on everything you do. I have seen people slam doors, upset chairs, bump into furniture without ever noticing that this way of doing things has an influence on their inner condition. Try this exercise of doing everything you do with love; one day, when you are upset or nervous, say to yourself, 'Ah, this is the moment to try out the exercise!'

Pick up an object, stroke it gently for a minute: you will feel something change inside you, a change in the currents. People do not know what to do to change their condition when they are upset and tense, they remain that way all day without doing anything about it. Instead of saying, 'I am running the risk of tearing down everything inside me, I must do something to change my rhythm, my gestures, my words...' they notice nothing. Their gestures are meaningless and their voice is like a machine gun! Then of course, they fall ill.

And the same thing for love, humans do not know how to love. To justify themselves they say, 'Master, you don't know human nature, it is terrible!' I don't know human nature! My answer is, if they have allowed their human nature to become so difficult to manage, they can also do something to control it and make it obey, to ennoble it. As they have never made an effort in the past, the nature they have formed is very difficult to change. That is the way to explain these things, rather than justifying oneself and making no effort because it is supposedly impossible to change. It is possible, if you exert yourself in a few years you will no longer be the same, you will be much happier for love will never leave you.

Love does not leave you, you are busy loving all the time and it is never tiring. You say you do not know this kind of love... whose fault is that, you have done nothing to know it! From now on say to yourself, 'The Master talks about love, another love, and that is the love I wish to know about.' Why always be sure that the truth is something other than what I give you? Reality you say, as if that explained everything... but there are realities and realities, dear brothers and sisters.

I am not saying that sexuality is not a reality, but why settle for an inferior, gross reality? There is another more subtle reality which has been grasped and lived by some who would for nothing on earth go back to living like the others again... they would refuse. And there are those whom nothing on earth can persuade to raise the degree of their love, they would rather neglect the great truths that could save them, and slide back down into animality; naturally their love cannot last more than a few minutes and then nothing is left but ashes. They say, 'Oh, it was so beautiful!' Maybe so, but it didn't last, the gold turned to lead. Nothing can tarnish the other kind of love, it remains gold forever.

I know that this love I am talking about is not easy to realize, because man has a certain heredity to combat. For thousands of years the human race has had their idea of love ingrained in their cells. It is extremely difficult to erase. But it is not because it takes more than a day to transform yourself that your concept of love should remain the same forever and that you should not believe what the Initiates say. If you cannot change, it means that you are either deformed or too weak, not that the Initiates deceive you. The lower your tendencies, the more you will need to satisfy them. But when you can develop other divine appetites and tendencies, then you will swim continuously in an ocean of cosmic Love; before you had only a few drops scattered around here and there (and what a lot of deception and unhappiness to go through to find them!) Now that you are plunged in the cosmic ocean, you can drink all you like, you don't need to go and steal a few drops of love from someone else.

I also know that what I am saying will be incomprehensible to most of you. Let them do their utmost and in a few incarnations they will be able to transform their love. No need to die! For those who have already worked in other incarnations, it is easier to be content with very little on the physical plane, but free to taste love in the higher regions, the spiritual plane. People who feel this way are rare.

How many young people inclined toward religion have taken a vow of chastity without knowing what they were getting into, without knowing themselves, without understanding human nature, and then one day the instincts and passions began to stir and overwhelmed them! What a tragedy! Yes, how many tragedies in convents, for both sexes. It is better to marry and have children than to torment oneself in a convent, to be the bride of Jesus supposedly, but committing adultery in one's imagination. It would be better in that case to leave the convent. God is much larger than we think, He never asks us to consecrate ourselves completely to Him if it means a life of torment. He would rather we had a wife or husband and children and did some good, than to live a disordered, disoriented life and poison the atmosphere with burning, ungratified desires.

There are saints who spent their lives in torment from their pent up sexual force, they never found peace, even at the last. St. Teresa of Avila was a very passionate girl, and so was St. Theresa of the Holy Child... no one knows what she went through, what temptations she fought. She was not as she is usually presented, a sweet little thing with a gentle submissive face... no, she was very strong and powerful by nature. I admire her, little St. Theresa, I love her, but I don't approve of the way she is represented in order to cover up reality.

Some saints retained their ardour until their last moment and this was not a bad thing, on the contrary. I have told you before that those who know how to use the sexual force are the richest and most privileged people because this force is a blessing. People want to commit suicide when they feel this ardour within them, they think they are damned. How could they understand, the Church never explains anything! In the Initiations the truth was presented differently: the sexual force is a gift of God, it is simply a question of knowing how to use it. Those who have a lot of coal or petrol in their cellars become multi-millionaires if they know what to do with it, and those who do not know are burned. The sexual force is energy, and man must learn how to use it to enlighten himself and make everything work inside him. Instead of letting himself feel guilty and discouraged and sad because he is ardent, he should hold his head high and say to himself, 'Ah, I am privileged, this energy will lead me to do the most extraordinary things.'

Brothers and sisters come to me complaining that they are upset, that they feel faint, unbalanced, and I ask them, 'Why did you stop loving? These troubles come from suppressing the love that is in you. When it is suppressed it goes to work and destroys everything. Love is a strong torrent. You did not know this because you have never been enlightened on the subject and now it has broken through the barriers. If you want to save yourself from torment, you must love! Love all beings, all creation. The energy must find another path leading to the heights. You repressed it because you were afraid, you didn't dare to love out of fear of being tempted, and now you are in worse shape than ever! Let your love manifest itself, but not the way everybody else does, give this energy another path. It is because you do not wish to love that this energy torments you. Love and you will be saved!'

Try to understand what I am saying, it is your salvation. Love! Love day and night, love all creatures, and there will be no time left for torment, you will be too busy! As it is now, the more miserly you are with your love, the more you want to break away; the more tightly you hold back and try to keep from loving, the more you are tempted. Be generous, for God's sake, and you will be saved! Give your love to all creatures. I found this secret and that is what I do. Of course I pass for an idiot most of the time, people say, 'Oh, the poor thing, his heart betrays him. We are more reasonable and intelligent, we do not waste our energy...' They have not discovered the secret of loving.

This theory of mine will not suit husbands or wives! The husbands will say, 'This is very dangerous, if my wife starts loving all men, what will happen to me? I want all her love for me alone.' And wives will say the same. But how many girls are smiling and graceful and lovely before marriage, and a short time afterwards they are silent and completely extinguished by the egoism of their husband. Husbands and wives are often personal and selfish, it is the reason for most of the trouble between them, but if the husband can learn to stretch his consciousness, he will be pleased when his wife loves the whole world! At the moment, if a wife smiles at someone else the husband is angry, which leads to endless discussions, arguments... and tragedy.

Egoism and personal interest are responsible for the traditions that prevent happiness. Humans must be more comprehensive, that is what will save them. This doesn't mean that a wife should sleep with other men, no, physically the wife belongs to her husband, it is in her heart that she can make room for everyone else, the angels, archangels, saints, prophets, poets, musicians, even film stars (she needs no encouragement from me!), and the husband cannot do anything to keep her from it. Women have always had a star that they love secretly and the husband also has a star (one or more) somewhere! He may say nothing about them to his wife, but when he sees them on the screen... Oh, my! He even thinks, 'If my wife were only like that!' but he has to make do with the one he has! If you knew what goes on in the minds of husbands and wives... but let us leave all that.

I revealed to you what happens in the subtle regions when a man and woman indulge their purely sexual, animal instincts. When they are enlightened and have a high ideal of love and know that they can serve the Kingdom of God with the energy of the sexual force, when they love each other and embrace with the idea of consecrating their love to divine realizations, then the vibrations are different, the emanations are different, everything between them is rich and beautiful and the angels themselves come and bring them gifts.

Love is not the same in all circumstances, it depends on the direction, the goal it has. The gestures may be the same, you always must approach the person you love, hold him and kiss and caress him. The difference is in what you put into your gestures. That is what counts! Someone says, 'Ah, I saw so and so kissing such and such a person,' and everyone condemns them. Heaven does not look at it that way, Heaven only cares about what was behind the kiss, whether there was something beautiful and pure between them, and if there was, Heaven rewards them. But try and explain to humans that it is not the gesture that counts! They only see the physical side.

If you put eternal, immortal, pure life and light into your love and the object of your love blossoms and evolves thanks to you, then it is real love, but if the one you love begins to decline, you should wonder, 'I am ruining this man or woman! Before he (or she) was splendid, and now he is a ruin!' and look for a way to repair the error of your ways as quickly as possible.

Your love should make the other person blossom forth, only then should you be happy and proud and thank Heaven for having succeeded in helping and protecting him. Usually people pay no attention to those things. Later they come to me and say, 'I love him, I love him!' I answer, 'Yes, but that kind of love is the same as the love you have for the chicken you put in the casserole: you love it, you devour it, and that is the end of it.' No, love should never devour, that is, ruin the other person. Love as I understand it is very different from what young people imagine.

Everyone talks of love in songs and films and books, it is a whole business! People sing about love, they glorify love, but that love is still too far down. I have been told that a whole scientific literature exists on sexuality, telling you exactly what to do and how, including unimaginable contortions. The physical side is all that matters! I realize it is necessary to speak certain words, but to sink down so far is not scientific as far as I am concerned, nor is it progress, on the contrary. That sex and instincts exist, I know and accept, but why not at least try to add a few ennobling elements to spiritualize them! I am not against sexual love, but when I see what goes on, I feel that mankind is sliding backwards out of the light; when the light disappears, man becomes prosaic and beastly with resulting ill effects on society such as degeneracy, criminality, exterminations, etc.

How many civilisations have disappeared because of degeneracy! If humans do not change their ways, our civilisation will also disappear. I know it is very difficult to change people, especially the young who put such emphasis on the physical side of love... how can it be otherwise? They must be taught the truth, that love is an immense and tremendously rich world which is not limited to the degrees we now know, and that the projects of Cosmic Intelligence are to bring humans nearer and nearer to the spiritual degrees of love...

In case there are boys and girls here today for the first time, I would like to add a few words that may be helpful. The rest of you may think my stories are shocking but in comparison they are nothing! If you knew what young people learn and hear and talk about and what they are busy doing, you would really be shocked. Little children of twelve or thirteen tell each other stories that are worse than mine!

One day I received a visit from a young girl, she was pretty and attractive and from her manners you could see that she had been well brought up. But she came to tell me how desperately unhappy she was: wherever she looked, on flowers, fruit, objects, even on the ceiling... she saw one thing only, a man's sexual organ. She was a practicing Catholic and felt guilty and rejected.

When I had heard her out, I began to laugh. While she looked at me in astonishment, I said to her, 'Listen to me. Would you allow me to explain something to you, and suggest a way out?' 'Oh, yes!' she said. And so I told her: There is nothing to worry about, nothing bad about what you told me, it is a natural and normal thing that can happen to anyone. There is no need to despair. Nature is the one who makes men and women feel this way to insure the preservation of the species. The thing is to know how to act about them, how to make use of these images, otherwise you'll always be in the state you are in now.

This is what to do: the next time you see this image on some object, instead of being upset observe it calmly (not too long because it might waken certain desires, and that will lead to something else). Become a bit philosophic about it, that is, begin to think about the Higher Intelligence that presided at the formation of these organs, meditate on these things and let yourself be amazed at an Intelligence that could create such perfection... in so doing you will forget all about the connotation the image has for you. If you let yourself think as you do now you will never be free. Instead, take this image as a starting point that can propel you all the way to the Spring; without a point of departure, how can you reach your high predestination? Use the image as a springboard but don't dwell on it for any length of time or you will be engulfed and lose yourself. The image is only a means to an end.

Unfortunately human beings do not know about going further and reflecting in wonderment, they don't know that this wonderment will be their salvation. They say, 'What is happening to me, it is too awful, too disgusting!' and they are lost. Get rid of those old concepts and do not say, 'How awful' anymore, but, 'How beautiful! How splendid, what intelligence! How did Nature ever do it!' And then, because of your awe and wonder, you will find your balance and be at peace. That is what I said to the young girl, and she was happy when she left.

God has done things very well, why should we mutilate His Creations? People treat sexuality as if God had not done things properly. But that is serious, that is punishable, we should be lost in admiration before everything that God has created, He knew why He created it, it is not for us to judge. What an odd philosophy humans have! You say it was meant to keep them pure and chaste... no, it pushes them into transgressing the laws of purity, things are presented as diabolical and this is what incites them to taste them!

Do you think that by calling sex ugly and disgusting people are kept from practicing it or being interested in it? People call it disgusting but wallow in it night and day! It doesn't prevent people, on the contrary... Baudelaire says that the greatest pleasure comes from doing something that makes you feel guilty; anything forbidden, anything criminal, increases your pleasure. Whether this is true or false, I will not discuss with you, I simply want you to know that to castigate sex is not the solution and never was. The only way is to think about it in another way.

The solution to love and sexuality, the only solution, is to change the way men and women consider each other. I say to the brothers: if you think of woman as a goddess, a divinity, you will not want to dirty her. The cause of disorder and passion is because of men not knowing how to think about women, and women not knowing how to consider men. A man who thinks of a woman as a female, a sort of Messalina, an object for his pleasure, his behaviour is predetermined: he will give in to desire; but if he thinks of her as a divinity, his feelings will make his comportment quite different.

Jesus said, *'According to your faith, be it unto you.'*[6] Yes, things *are* according to the way you think they are: it is the magic that has never been explained. We think we can change the way we love without changing the way we think about the object of our love. No, no, love is extremely difficult to transform. But if you can change your way of thinking about someone or something, your feelings and tendencies and actions are affected. I consider woman a divinity. You say, 'Poor fellow, how wrong you are! If you only knew!' Do you really think I do not know? But I do not wish to think of her that way, I do not choose to know what she is nor what she can be like and that helps me, I do it purposely. If you think I do not know what women are like! I have every reason to think of them as dreadful, but I want to think of them as divine for *my* sake. I benefit from thinking of woman as a divinity! This is a whole philosophy in itself.

Years ago, a doctor came to see me, an elderly paunchy man and he began to talk about women. Do you know what he said? He said, 'A woman is nothing but a vagina.' I was aghast. Tell me, what good does it do to think that way? In part it is true of course, human beings have intestines and all sorts of things that are far from aesthetic, but those intestines, that body, is not the man or woman. Humans get everything mixed up! A physical body has different parts to function with, but the man, the woman, are not as they appear physically, they are beings who think and feel, who have a soul and a spirit.

What joy can men derive from thinking of women as organs? Men are not experts in psychology, they don't know that our thoughts influence our inner state. What interests me is to know precisely that: how everything I think reflects on me. For that reason I prefer to think of woman as a divinity. You say, 'But it's not true!' Perhaps you are right to reason that way, but I am not interested in that kind of reasoning, I find it dangerous. Living as I do with my illusions (living with lies if you will) makes me the happiest of men. And furthermore they are not lies: I believe that women are divine, an aspect of the Divine Mother, and this gives me a joy, a happiness, that are unbelievable! If I thought the way that doctor spoke, do you think I could come and lecture to you? I would not come to see you, nor talk to you, nor anything else.

You too should change your thinking. Men should change the opinion they have of women and women should change their opinion of men, otherwise the doors of their evolution will be closed. They will not be able to advance.

Very few people know that their way of thinking about others can affect their evolution. In the past when a disciple had a teacher, to him this Master was a divinity, a god, the disciple progressed because of his way of thinking about his Master. The fact that the Master was not exceptional in any way is unimportant, the disciple was able to advance, because of his way of thinking he became something extraordinary. Now people are prosaic, disrespectful, gross, and they wonder why they do not improve. It is because they disregard the means of improving!

When I was in India I heard this story. Among the disciples of a certain Master was a lad who revered his Master to such an extent that he thought of him as a divinity. One day, the disciples came running to the Master saying that the young disciple was walking on the water! The Master summoned him and asked how he did it. 'Oh, it's quite easy, Master,' said the disciple. 'I simply pronounce your name.' 'Very good,' thought the Master, 'I will do the same.' He rowed to the middle of the lake, stepped out onto the water, and... drowned! The Master drowned and the disciple walked on the water! It was not the name that was important you see, but the fervent love with which the disciple pronounced it.

Everything depends on the way you consider things. Maybe your good opinion of me will enable you to perform miracles that I would not be able to! But as long as you think of me as an idiot, it will be I who will perform the miracles, not you. I too have a name to pronounce... which one? No, the name is not your concern... in any case it is not my own.

What I am explaining is that reality is the magic side of things. The only science that ever interested me is the science of magic, white magic. Everything is magic, a conversation, a glance, a gesture, food, love, a walk. People are horrified to hear the word magic, but whether they know it or not they are plunged in magic all the time.[7] It is the only science, all the others stem from it, alchemy, astrology, the Kabala are branches of magic. Magic is everywhere. When you kiss someone, you release magic forces that are extremely powerful: you use these forces without realizing that you are playing with matches and are liable to light a fire by throwing them around left and right. People don't like the word magic but they use it all the time... like Mr Jourdain in Molière's 'Bourgeois Gentilhomme,' who was unaware that he was speaking prose.

Dear God, to have to explain things that are so elementary, so simple and clear... things you should already know and be working on in silence, but I am always obliged to talk about them because you do not yet know how to work. I must explain, but I promise you, I am longing for the moment when I need not talk anymore, when we can work together in silence. I am interested in the work itself, the creative work of realizing by thought all kinds of creations, and tossing them out into space. During the conferences I talk and talk and talk, but nothing is clear to you, because instead of going to work, you remain passive, always waiting for more explanations, as if you expect someone to come and feed you... no one will do that unless you are ill in the hospital. If you are in good health, you are expected to feed yourself.

There is still something to say, but I hesitate because it will seem odd and I do not think you will understand. However, I will go ahead. Let us say you are a woman and you are holding your beloved in your arms. You call him by name, dear so and so, dear Tom, dear John, you say his name so that his personality will rejoice over how much you love him. In that way all your energies are engulfed by his personality. Now suppose both of you know about the personality and the individuality, and you both have a knowledge of the Initiatic Science: when you embrace him, you say, 'O Heavenly Father!' thus making your lover the conductor of your energy to the Heavenly Father. If when he kisses you he calls you the Divine Mother, his energy will also go heavenward. This is knowledge that humans do not have. They serve each other's personalities, and as the personality has subterranean roots, all their energies go below. The individuality which has its roots above steers everything toward Heaven.[8]

If they want to help each other and have a beneficial effect on each other, men and women should invoke the Heavenly Father and the Divine Mother during their embraces, and their energies will go to Heaven. It is simple, but very difficult to make humans accept this idea. They have their old habits ingrained in them, and they repeat and repeat them, always satisfying their personality and doing nothing for the poor starving individuality. The personality receives quantities of food all day, it is even sated, but it will turn against you because gratitude is not in its nature.

For years I have been observing how the personality and the individuality manifest themselves in humans, and I am convinced that no matter what you do for the personality it is never thankful. A woman gives everything she has to the man she loves, and what does he do? He goes off with someone else. Why? Because although she satisfied him sexually, she was unable to nourish the other side in him which is sublime, the other nature that never forgets and is eternally grateful. Afterwards the poor woman laments, 'I gave him everything I had, and see how he treats me!' Yes, because she nourished the side of him that is ungrateful.

On the subject of personality and individuality, I will add a few words. When a man gives free rein to a purely personal, selfish love, it is clear that his organs function independently of him, they are outside his control. He is aware of this, but can do nothing about it, other forces take over, he is there simply as an observer! When it is a spiritual love that you feel, you know it is you, that is, your soul and spirit, your individuality, that are in control and are nourished. Maybe it was only a look, a presence, a whiff of perfume, but you are happy and filled with joy, knowing that you yourself, your higher Self, has breathed and been fed, not other forces enjoying themselves through you.

But humans never observe themselves, they plunge into pleasure regardless, and because the physical body is satisfied with the few crumbs it receives, they imagine that they are happy and satisfied, they don't see that the void is still there in their soul and spirit. If they identify themselves with the physical body, it is enough for the body to be satisfied. If they were not identified with the personality, they would understand that whilst the physical body is sated, asleep and snoring, they themselves are starving because their soul and spirit, that is, their individuality, has received nothing at all. Yes, that is the extraordinary science of the personality and the individuality.

There are more things to say, but let us leave them for another conference. Remember this idea that you must love, love without ceasing, that is what will bring your salvation. Try to reach a higher degree each time. You shouldn't expect all manifestations of sexuality to cease at once, but if you have decided to go up into the higher regions, it will not be long before you see that what you receive is beyond all the pleasures you tasted before and paid for so dearly in health, beauty, and peace.

The whole world is interested only in love; a film or book that are not about love will not succeed. I too think about nothing but love... why should I be different? Hypocrites say, 'Love doesn't interest me...' but I do not believe them. For me nothing is really interesting but love, only there is another way of understanding love. It is written in the Gospels that God is Love. Why abandon that love? If God is love we should know His love, we should live that love. To know that love, we must go beyond certain limitations, certain errors that detain us. Only love can heal us, strengthen us, beautify us, enlighten us, and that is why we must love day and night according to the forms and rules of the Teaching.

The sad thing is that when you speak of love, people think of physical love, carnal love. When I speak to you of love, I am thinking of another love, spiritual love. Physical love doesn't interest me, I have another concept of love, and that is what must be explained so as to avoid misunderstandings.

Love is an exchange, and exchanges exist on other planes beside the physical, they can take place between two people at a distance through a look, a thought, a word, without ever embracing or touching. Nor is it necessary to make exchanges only with humans who are often ugly, sickly, and gloomy... you can also make exchanges with heavenly beings, celestial creatures who are beautiful, pure, full of light! But if you accept love as everyone else does, then of course, nothing wonderful will happen to make you bloom.

When I speak of love I mean love that is life, light and beauty, an exchange with divine creatures. That is the love I think about night and day, and this love brings me blessings. If I thought about the other kind of love, I too would have to practice it: the thought leads to the act. Think about something, pretty soon you will be doing it.[9] Someone who thinks about putting his hand in someone else's pocket to steal finds himself doing it one day. That is how pickpockets are made! And if you think about kissing someone, one day you will be surprised to find yourself doing it!

Do not think about things if you do not want them realized, because they will be realized, that is what you must understand. No one can withstand the laws of Nature. If you think certain thoughts, sooner or later you will have to do as those thoughts suggest. Other thoughts are realized in another way, for instance, instead of wanting to kiss a man or woman, why not want to embrace the sun? No danger is involved, the sun is too far away!

You see there are different kinds of love. But this philosophy is so remote for humans, they will not accept it, they will say, 'What? Love the sun instead of loving a man or woman? That's stupid!' No, they are the ignorant ones, they don't know that love is spread about everywhere in the atmosphere, in the oceans and rivers, on mountains and rocks, on the grass, flowers and trees, all over the earth and, specially in the sun. Love is a cosmic energy most extraordinarily abundant and diversified.

But because people don't know this, they are content with a few drops of dew somewhere on the physical body... and that is so little, so insignificant. That is where all the trouble starts. The Initiates have discovered that love is spread about in profusion everywhere and that if they develop certain very subtle faculties within themselves, they can capture it.

I have told you about seeing a plant in a friend's house at Nice that was suspended in air; instead of having its roots in the ground, it drew its nourishment from the atmosphere. In other words, this plant had a different constitution than other plants, a higher constitution. Humans do not know that they are like that plant, that they too can draw love from the atmosphere and from the sun. That is why they have never developed their higher centres. In India, in Tibet, yogis work to awaken these centres, the chakras, and are able to draw upon the energy that is spread around everywhere in Nature. They don't need to look for women, they are happy and satisfied in the midst of plenty.

You see, there are still many things to say on the subject of love. People don't even know what it is yet, and the things they say about it are unbelievable. Love is a force, an energy, a fluid, a quintessence that you can find everywhere. God never meant love to be limited to certain places on the human body. God is more generous, larger than that. He distributed love everywhere. Those who are ignorant and look for it only in men or women are not always able to find it, but the Initiates who look for it elsewhere are never without it! For thousands of years humans have been told what to believe and now they cannot believe it possible to live and love without having roots beneath the ground.

I am not so naive as to think that what I am saying applies to everyone. No, amongst the millions and millions of human beings there are barely two or three who are prepared to understand what love really is and live that love. That is the sad truth. But that is no reason not to enlighten those few people so that they can acquire courage, confidence and strength, and never doubt, never hesitate, never turn back again into the crowd of ordinary men who are weak, primitive and sensual. I am speaking, not for the world at large, but for the few who are looking for new ways, new paths.

No, I am not stupid enough to think that everyone will rush into these new ideas... besides it would be dangerous if they did, doctors would say, 'Ah, you see we were right!' Because what they have determined, the advice they give, is based on research carried out on the masses, on the majority, and when they say, 'Unless you give issue to the sexual forces you will be ill,' implying that a boy must find relief with a woman, they are right. But they have never studied the lives of the minority of Sages and Initiates to see how successful they are and why they are in perfect health. If they did, they would have to correct their conclusions and admit that for some people it is one thing, for others it is another. At the moment they put everyone in the same basket, which is wrong. Fortunate are those who are ready to live with universal love!

Ah, what a temptation to go on, because there is no subject more important than this one, the subject of love.[10] Besides, there is no one who is not listening, everybody's eyes and ears are wide open! If you speak on other subjects, they go to sleep. Yes, 'Love, love, you have us in your grip...' is true, is it not?

Toulouse, 8th February, 1971

Notes

1. See *In Spirit and in Truth*, Izvor Coll. n° 235, chap. 1: 'The framework of the Universe'.
2. See *Hope for the World: Spiritual Galvanoplasty*, Izvor Coll. n° 214, chap. 8: 'The Solar Nature of Sexual Energy'.
3. See *Love and Sexuality*, Complete Works, vol. 14, chap. 27: 'Youth and the Problem of Love'.

4. See *The Book of Divine Magic,* Izvor Coll. n° 226, chap. 2: 'The Magic Circle of the Aura'.

5. See *Harmony and Health,* Izvor Coll. n° 225, chap. 8: 'How to Become Tireless', *Les deux arbres du Paradis,* Complete Works, vol. 3, chap. 4: 'La puissance magique des gestes et du regard'.

6. See *Love Greater Than Faith,* Izvor Coll. n° 239, chap. 5: 'Let it be done for you according to your appreciation'.

7. See *The Book of Divine Magic,* Izvor Coll. n° 226, chap. 10: 'We All Work Magic'.

8. See *'You Are Gods',* Synopsis Coll., Part II, chap. 1: 'Lower nature and higher nature'.

9. See *Harmony,* Complete Works, vol. 6, chap. 6: 'How Thought is Materialized on the Physical Plane'.

10. See *Love and Sexuality,* Complete Works, vol. 14 and vol. 15.

Part IV

REALIZATION

Chapter One

THE SPRING

The thought I read a while ago from the Master Peter Deunov contained an idea which I consider most important. I will therefore go over it once more: 'When you are a spring, alive and flowing, everyone can hear you singing from afar; when you are but a well, a reservoir, you are calm and peaceful, no more. The life of a well is beautiful but the life of a spring is the most beautiful of all. A spring waters the land, the trees, the grass, the flowers, its pure water quenches the thirst of the weary traveller.'

We have talked about the spring, not only little mountain springs, but the much more powerful, unique and live spring that is the sun. As far as I am concerned it is not a well or a reservoir that I would oppose to the spring, but something far worse, a swamp. There is fresh water in a well or a reservoir, cool and drinkable water, but the water in a swamp is filthy and poisonous to drink. If you can discern the deep significance of the spring and the swamp, you will see the magic in them and you will understand many things.

In observing humans, you see by their attitudes and reasoning that they never think about the spring that vibrates, wells up and flows. They answer, 'What can thinking about a spring do for us?' They may be very learned and intelligent, but they miss the essential point, they don't see that their whole lives, all their actions, depend on the idea, the image they have in their minds: the dead image of a swamp or the vibrant creative image of a spring, the sun. Everything depends on that, I have observed man for years and have come to the conclusion that everything depends on the choice he makes between the spring and the swamp. By his choice he demonstrates his understanding of life.

People complain that nothing works out for them... why? Because in their mind and soul they do not put divine things (like the spring) in first place, so that the flowing water can purify inside them and water their seedlings. Nothing in their feelings and desires denotes any interest in a centre, a spring, a source, the sun, the Spirit, Love. They have settled for insignificant things, they do not even try to understand and prefer wading around in stagnant polluted water crawling with insects. They make fun of the philosophy of the Initiates that is so insistent on the importance, the magic, of linking with the spring, but why think that something mouldy and decrepit will be of any help?

Some people wonder why we go to the sunrise... it is symbolic, a proof that we depend on the sun for our existence and must link ourselves to it at the source.[1] Try and convince so-called intelligent people to get up and watch the sun rise! They prefer darkness and polluted, dead things, and then wonder why they are in trouble. The reason is that they hold on to their inner impurities, they don't follow the example of the spring, they don't flow as the spring does. The first time I spoke in France,[2] it was on the subject of the spring; I began with the spring and it is still flowing.

Sometimes I ask people, 'Have you ever seen a spring, a source? Can you describe what happens around it?' 'Of course,' they say, but they have not really observed things. I pursue my questions. 'What is there near the spring?' 'Plants, vegetation, green things.' 'What else?' 'Insects, animals, birds.' 'What else?' 'People have built their homes nearby.' 'Very good. But when the spring goes dry, do you know what happens? First of all the grass goes, then the animals, then the human beings, and the last ones to go are the trees. Do you think you understand that?' 'Of course, it's simple.' 'Well, why did you let your spring go dry?' 'What spring? I don't understand...'[3]

You see, they do not understand. We think we understand but it is only in appearance. I continue, 'I mean the spring flowing inside you... why have you let that spring dry up?' 'But what spring?' 'Your spring is dry because you have no love. You were disappointed, cheated or abandoned by someone, and now you say, 'I am through with being generous, good, charitable: people don't deserve it.' Your spring has dried up! Of course, because no one cheats you anymore you think you have gained, but the truth is you have lost, lost everything. The spring must not dry up, no matter what! No amount of harm that people do to you is worth giving up the blessed spring that flows within you, bringing you all that is good, cleansing you and restoring you to health.'

Humans need this philosophy of the spring, the most marvellous, most truthful of all philosophies. A person is hurt and as a result, stops loving... when that happens he is already dead. What does he gain if he is dead? Human reasoning is extraordinary! And they want me to learn from them? No, I would rather go and find a spring and listen to it, I would rather stay near it, watching it, touching it, talking to it, thinking about the other spring, the sun, and all the other springs in the universe up to the real Spring which is God. I would rather link myself to that Spring and understand the essential. You ask, 'What can you learn from a spring?' Everything.

Years ago I read 'Siddhartha' by Hermann Hesse. You know it no doubt, the story of a young brahman, Siddhartha, who, after living for a long time in study, meditation and prayer, suddenly throws himself into pleasure and debauchery. One day, in despair, disgusted with himself, he comes to a river, and stays there on the shore listening to it, watching it. Little by little he finds everything he had ever sought in his wanderings, all the Mysteries of life and death. The river teaches him understanding.

Many people learned understanding from Nature by contemplating the stars and listening to the wind.[4] Among the Druids were many great Initiates living their lives in harmony with the cosmic forces, receiving their revelations from the collective soul of the mountains, trees, lakes, springs, birds, and animals.

You must understand that the magic side to this image of, the spring is that your entire life should be based on the Spring, or God, whose perfect earthly representative is the sun. You should work on this all your life, learning to imitate the sun so as to warm people and vivify them, to quench their thirst and ressuscitate them. You say, 'But that's impossible! It's too unrealizable, too stupid.' If you think that way, you haven't understood. The important thing is not to have an ideal that is easy to realize, but to do the inner work on yourself that will transform you. The sun is immense, powerful beyond belief, and to become that great and powerful is impossible of course. But on his own level man can become a sun. Instead of always grabbing, instead of being a swamp and dirtying everything, he can learn to give, to purify, to vivify others. The idea is not utopian, it is realizable, you have only to *want* to study, to experiment, to verify the possibilities.

Unfortunately I find that here in the Brotherhood most of the brothers and sisters have not understood the magic power, the extraordinary science of the spring. For years I have been talking of nothing else and if they had understood they would have learned how to realize something pure and vital in themselves. If they are still somber, closed, rigid, it means they have not understood this Teaching. They want to arrange their lives by means of the swamp; a swamp is not capable of arranging anything, it is good only for larvae, toads and slimy things groveling in the mud.

The inhabitants of stagnant water are obliged to breathe and swallow refuse from all the other inhabitants and it is the same for humans: the world is a huge swamp with people crawling around like insects, obliged to absorb one another's excrement. Anyone who manages to climb out is rewarded with a whiff of purity, but the others are strangled by it. The atmosphere in a big city is the same, if you were clairvoyant you would see how humans devour each other, no one knows how to get out of the swamp even for a minute. Yet they make fun of the solar philosophy! So much the worse for them, let them stay where they are. What else can I say? One day they will be forced to understand.[5]

The Master Peter Deunov chose the image of a reservoir: he was kinder than I. I choose the image of the swamp because it is so clear, and anyone can understand the image of the spring, the sun.

What conclusion can be drawn from this? That all human problems, misunderstandings, trouble and suffering, come from the fact that man is not linked with Heaven, the Spring, or if he is, it is only for a minute or two and then he turns back to the swamp. It is not my purpose to make those who are here angry (these are generalities) but instead of being linked to this Spring that purifies, heals, enlightens, people prefer to go and link themselves with a swamp (a swamp can be a man or a woman, a group of people); they drink that water and prefer the swamp to the spring out of fear of the swamp-dwellers' opinion: if the toads in the swamp objected to them, what would become of them?

I am pointing out the way, but it is up to you to decide; I am not here to please you, I am here to tell you the truth. I know it is not pleasant to hear, but if you could realize instead of being upset that if I say nothing, one day you will be twice, three times, a hundred times worse off. Because ignorance leads to trouble. If you have knowledge, at least you can escape down the backstairs and leave your enemy at a loss.

Reflect on the two images of the spring and the swamp. When finally you decide to love, to make a sacrifice, to help others and give instead of taking, it will mean that the spring is flowing, and once it starts to flow, the flowers and trees will grow, birds will sing, and wonderful spirits will come and install themselves in your mind and heart and will. The spring will feed them and you will become a rich country with a flourishing civilisation. Because the spring is flowing! That symbolism is what you must learn to understand.

When the spring is dry, no one stays near it; when the spring stops flowing in man, there is nothing left, no poetry or music, no joy, nothing... he is a void, a desert, because there is no water, no love. At the moment there are nothing but deserts walking around in the world, which explains the miserable state it is in, the distress and emptiness people feel. The world's inhabitants may be highly intelligent, but they have let their spring go dry, it never occurs to them to give, to radiate, to love. When I see people in whom the spring is dry or has never flowed, I know that they will be miserable. Why? Because nothing divine will come near them, no angel, no spirit, no beauty, no splendour, nothing.

Fortunate are those who have understood this and want to change! They will have heard, they will have found in what I said today the explanation they sought; the image of the swamp and the spring explains everything: if you are stagnant, if your life is without enthusiasm or inspiration, without joy, you know that you have let the spring inside you go dry! You didn't notice, you were too busy criticizing others, but that is what happened. Now leave the others alone and turn on your spring and let it flow. If it is stopped up, clean it and the water will flow. It must flow because man was born to become a spring, God sent man to live on earth to be a spring.

But he has let the filth of the years accumulate inside and his spring is stopped up, it is a desert, a void. Nothing is worse than being a desert.

Are you beginning to understand what the image of the spring means? The spring is life, it is love! Love is all-powerful, love creates inspiration and joy and that, dear brothers and sisters, is the greatest truth. I know that in spite of the great truths you have heard over the years, many of you are in a sad state: it is because you don't know how to work, you have no method of working. No matter what humans hear, no matter how glorious the truths they are given to help them transform their desert, they pay no attention, they retain nothing. If at least they wrote down one truth and looked at it every day... but no, an hour later the talks are forgotten. If they refuse to understand or retain anything you tell them, it is their own fault. They are predestined to a life in the desert!

I speak very often about the spring, I know, but you need to have things repeated. The sun rose yesterday but that was for yesterday... it must rise again today! Flowing water may appear to be the same always but it is not, it is always fresh. That is why I keep repeating over the years, 'Think every day about making the spring flow! Open it, clean it, and let the water flow so that you will be the fertile ground that royalty will want to come and visit to taste the fruit in your garden!' I repeat again: why have you not planted anything in the rich ground you have inside, why have you never harvested anything? What is your brain, your mind? The best earth there is, and it is this earth that you must cultivate, you must take these seeds and plant them and spray them with water.

Think about the spring, the true spring, the source, the Sun. Have the ideal of becoming a sun yourself no matter how tremendous, how unrealizable it may seem and in a few years time, no matter what you may appear to be, inside you will be a sun.

Have a heart as pure as crystal
A mind as luminous as the sun
A soul as vast as the universe
A spirit as powerful as God and
One with Him.

You have this formula given by Master Peter Deunov, it is buried somewhere amongst your papers. You say it isn't possible to become vast as the universe but what do you know about it? An Initiate knows how to become so vast that clairvoyants can see him in trees, lakes, and mountains, they see him hard at work all over the earth. That is his reason for being here. Yes, a human being can be everywhere at once, but only if he thinks he can be, only if he believes it. The great Initiates have a formula that helps them to develop themselves in order to participate in the work of Cosmic Intelligence. With it they penetrate into the bowels of the earth, the depths of the ocean, the heights of the atmosphere. Physically they are as they appear, but their spirit participates in all kinds of construction going on in the universe.

One day humans will start to study these things and they will understand that the possibilities of the spirit are infinite and endless. For the moment they do not understand, it doesn't interest them. They shrink back voluntarily, they don't dare go beyond certain limits (why should they go further than their fathers before them, their grandfathers, great-grandfathers and great-great-grandfathers?) This way of thinking limits and weakens them. They choose to remain small and miserable, no one will ever convince me of the contrary. You say, 'No, they hope, they wish...' It may appear so, but deep down in his beliefs and concepts, man doesn't dare believe that he can become great. He hopes he can, but it is not enough to hope.

And so, dear brothers and sisters, meditate on this image of the Spring as it feeds and waters the whole universe.

Sèvres, 10th April, 1966

Notes
1. See *Méditations au lever du soleil,* Brochure n° 323.
2. See *The Second Birth,* Complete Works, vol. 1, chap. 1: 'The Second Birth'.
3. See *The Mysteries of Fire and Water,* Izvor Coll. n° 232, chap. 4: 'Civilization, a Product of Water'.
4. Op. cit., chap. 19: 'A Treasury of Pictures'.
5. See *On the Art of Teaching – from the Initiatic Point of View,* Complete Works, vol 29, chap. 4: 'On the Living Knowledge'.

Chapter Two

FASTING

You know that when you eat, your system absorbs what it needs and tries to get rid of what is foreign or harmful to it. The system is not able to do this eliminating when it has been overcharged or when the food it is given contains too many impurities. The waste matter then accumulates in the different organs, especially in the intestines.

How can you distinguish pure food from impure food? Food that putrifies rapidly and leaves a lot of waste matter in the system is not pure, even when washed and cooked, it is still impure. Food that does not decay rapidly, such as fruit which keeps fresh for a long time, and vegetables that are full of solar energy, is pure.[1]

Even when it is pure, food leaves behind a lot of waste matter in the system, which is why the Initiates advise fasting from time to time to rid the physical body of impurities. Fasting is advocated by Nature... animals know instinctively that they must fast and eat grass to purge themselves when they are sick. When your furniture is covered with dust, you wipe it off, but when it is a question of cleaning your own organism at least once a week so that the millions of workers, the cells of your body, will be able to rest... you do nothing. Sometimes you have a fever, a runny nose and eyes, eruptions on your skin: it is a purification. Humans are too stubborn to purify themselves and the organs are compelled to do it for them.

I advise fasting twenty-four hours each week, for twenty-four hours take nothing but hot boiled water, nothing else. During that time you work spiritually, thinking about the higher beings, listening to good music and reading inspiring books, to purify your thoughts and feelings as well as the physical body. If you do that regularly you will ascertain that the waste matter you eliminate has no odor... do not be shocked, think of me for the moment as a doctor: if the waste matter discharged by your intestines and perspiration has a strong unpleasant odour, you can be sure that you are either ill or going to be, physically or psychically. You reply that odours depend on the food you take in... no, if you watch yourself carefully you will see that when you have been anxious and overwrought, angry or jealous, the odour changes. One's odour is very revealing.

I receive many letters (especially from women) saying, 'I am willing to fast, but when I do, I become ugly!' Yes, perhaps in the beginning, but that only proves the presence of a lot of refuse that must be got rid of. At the start you may also have headaches, palpitations, fainting spells, but there is nothing to be afraid of, it is natural. No one has ever died from fasting occasionally, but thousands and thousands die from overeating! It may be new and upsetting for the system to begin with, but it is only momentary and in fact a good sign. If you can stand a little discomfort and keep on with your fast, you will see that in a day or two the inner disorder gives way to an extraordinary tranquility.

You must not judge fasting by the first effects, there is no danger involved, on the contrary, people who are disturbed are the very ones who need to fast most, the disturbance is caused by the superabundant waste matter being discharged into the bloodstream by the cleansing. People think that fasting weakens them and gives them an unhealthy look, which could be true at the beginning but when you become lighter, your skin clears up and you are more pleasant to look at! If you don't know the language of Nature, you can be scared to death by a little discomfort. You think, 'With these palpitations, I may die, I feel weak!' and start eating again, congesting your system just as it was beginning to emerge from all the encumbrance. As the disturbances cease when you resume eating, you conclude that you were right in interrupting the fast, but it is not so.

People who are seriously interested in fasting must learn to think differently. If they feel upset they must pay no attention but keep on until the disturbances stop, which will be shortly. The disturbances are the result of Nature trying to rid the organism of waste matter, and the best thing is to wait until that is done. By refusing to wait, you make the same mistake as people who take pills to stop a fever. It may make them feel better for the moment, but to bring a fever down that way paves the way for a much more serious illness. It is better to let the system react by itself. When the system is overcharged, it reacts by doing everything it can to eliminate waste matter, and this process of dissolving or eliminating the waste is what gives you a temperature, it is the inner cleansing that causes it. How can you help the system do this cleansing? By drinking water, boiling hot water. Several cups in succession will bring the fever down immediately: the canals dilate and the blood circulates freely, bearing the waste matter out of the body through the normal channels...

Hot water is essential when you are fasting. Bring it to a boil to kill the germs, and let it settle. When you wash dishes in cold water, the plates are still greasy; hot water is also needed to dissolve grease in the organism, it dissolves substances that cold water leaves intact, and draws them out of the body through the pores and kidneys, etc., and you are rejuvenated! You might drink hot water every day before breakfast, it is an excellent remedy against arteriosclerosis, rheumatism, etc.

Hot water may not be appetizing at first, but little by little you will begin to feel so well that it becomes a pleasure. Hot water is an extraordinary remedy, but it is so simple, so cheap, that no one takes it seriously. One of the brothers cured himself that way of an illness that his doctor had been unable to cure. When the brother went back to the doctor, cured, the latter said, 'Yes, I know hot water works miracles in many cases, but how can I charge a consultation fee for prescribing hot water?'

When you fast, your etheric body[2] goes to work to bring the physical body purer, more subtle elements, it watches over the physical body and restores its energy when needed; fasting makes the etheric body work, during which time the physical body rests. If the fast lasts too long, the etheric body is overworked, it has more than it can handle alone. The physical body and the etheric body are partners and if only one does the work, the balance is disturbed.

I have told you that one of the most important rules of nutrition is to stop eating *before* you are full. Why? Because if you get up from the table still hungry, your system reacts to this insufficiency and the etheric body supplies what is lacking... that is why if you wait a little, you are no longer hungry and you feel much better than if you had eaten your fill. Always leave the table slightly hungry. People think it is better to eat a lot, but nothing makes you grow old faster than loading the stomach.

When I say to leave the table hungry, I mean a very slight hunger. If you deprive the system of something it needs over a long period of time, the etheric body is not able to take care of it, but if you eat a little less than you are used to, you will feel lighter and better disposed toward life because of the added etheric element. If you eat too much you will feel heavy and sleepy. Why? Because sleep is necessary while the etheric body rids the system of the burdensome food. If the surplus must be removed, why add it in the first place?

You think that what I am saying is not very important and is certainly not an Initiatic subject, but if you leave the table each time feeling slightly empty, if you fast and drink hot water from time to time, you will see tremendous benefits even in your spiritual life.

I will add a few words on the way you should end a fast that has lasted several days... if you eat normally at once it can be fatal. The first day, take a few cups of bouillon; the next day, soup and crackers; the third day begin to eat normally again, but not too much. In that way you risk nothing; after such a fast you are filled with new, subtle and wonderful feelings and revelations, you feel and look younger, freer, as if something heavy in your system has been burned away with the impurities. It is fear and ignorance that have kept humans from fasting and being regenerated.

Sèvres, 30th January, 1945

Notes
1. See *The Yoga of Nutrition,* Izvor Coll. n° 204, chap. 5: 'Vegetarianism'.
2. See *'Et il me montra un fleuve d'eau de la vie',* Synopsis Coll., p. 108-109, p. 126-129, p. 300-301.

Chapter Three

WASHING

1

When I ask the question, 'What do you do when you wake up in the morning?' sometimes I get this answer, 'I light the lamp, I turn on the light and then I pray, meditate or read.' 'All this in bed?' 'Yes.' And I am amazed.

Today, I will give you some advice that may seem simple but is terribly important. When you wake up in the morning, the first thing to do is light the lamp if it is dark, and then get up immediately. The second thing to do is wash. Before praying, before fixing breakfast for your husband and children, before doing anything at all, you must wash your face and hands, being careful not to touch your eyes before washing. It says in the Kabala that as soon as a man falls asleep, an evil spirit attaches itself to his physical body and is still attached to his hands and face when he awakens. We must not do anything before removing the fluidic layers left by this impure spirit.

The first task for the disciple during Initiation is to purify himself, and purification by water is one of the best methods. Physical water corresponds to the water in space, the etheric medium which can purify his astral and mental bodies. When you wash, do it consciously, for washing is as sacred a rite as eating. Your gestures must be deliberate and harmonious: in the etheric realm there is a very subtle order of the particles, and gestures that are brusque disturb this order. Observe yourself and you will see that if you do things hurriedly you feel demagnetized.

When you wash, concentrate on the feeling of freshness the water leaves on your skin, it will clear your thoughts and make way for better ideas to come to you. Be conscious that your hands are doing something sacred, say to yourself, 'In the name of the immortal and eternal love, in the name of the immortal and eternal wisdom in which we live and have our being, may this water deliver me from impurity.' Instead of feeling upset or worried, you will feel peaceful and tranquil.

Water has the property of absorbing, it takes on the same colours as the land it traverses. Initiates have always used water as a purifier, they know how powerful it is; on the etheric plane it also has absorbing properties, and Initiates use it to wash away psychic impurities. By pronouncing formulas, by using fragrant perfumes or other ingredients to exalt the water, you make it even more effective.

But to become pure through the help of water, you have to link yourself with the spiritual, cosmic water above; unless you make the link with that water the impure fluids will not be washed away completely.

In the Book of Genesis it says that God separated the waters above from the waters below.[1] The waters above represent the magic agent through which the world was created, the cosmic astral light, the primordial 'water' in which all beings are immersed and nourish themselves with. We live in this cosmic water as fish in the sea, but the impurities that obstruct our inner openings keep most of us from being nourished and vivified by it. Water envelops us on all sides. The child immersed in liquid in its mother's womb is very significant: the water below is the reflection of the water above, it contains the same elements and forces as the higher water, but alone the great Magi know how to draw upon it.

Water is the universal medium that carries the fluidic elements from one region to another; the water that comes down from the highest mountains is therefore impregnated with heavenly fluids. When you drink water, you are influenced by the place it comes from: never drink water that flows near a slaughter-house, cemetery or wash-house, always make sure it comes from a place that is pure.

Water is the great transmitter. Some plants cannot release their healing virtues unless they are placed in water, the water makes them effective. Water is subject to influences from its environment: if it is exposed to the sun, it will have entirely different properties than if it is exposed to the moon, the influences are different. In ancient times they believed that water exposed to the moon was not good to drink; at night they covered all receptacles for fear of the evil influence of the night spirits.

Water absorbs and transmits. When we drink water, it tells our cells the story of its travels, we can learn the mysteries of life on earth from water if we drink slowly, consciously thinking about where it has been.

Mediums use water to enable them to see into the invisible world, and it is well known that people who live near lakes and rivers become clairvoyant. The Ancients made spherical receptacles that they filled with pure water to make the spirits of the invisible world appear to them. If we know what to do, water can purify us and permit us to see things in all their clarity. Life is like water, when it is agitated and troubled nothing is clear but when it is calm, it reflects Heaven.

Suppose you wish to purify yourself where there is no water. Imagine a feeling of freshness, as if drops of water were falling on you and carrying off all your impurity. This spiritual bath is most effective because as I said, the real water is not physical, inside man is a spring of living water, and that is what Jesus meant when he said, *'From his belly shall flow rivers of living water...'*[2] Physical water is nothing but a means of communication with spiritual water.

When you are overcome with sadness for some reason and don't know how to get rid of it, listen to water, look at flowing water if only water from the tap: in a few minutes you will feel better. Water soothes the solar plexus. Or plunge your hands in water – cold or hot, in a few minutes you will have the impression of having your burden lifted. Wash your hands with soap once, twice, ten times, consciously washing your etheric hands as well.

As you wash your hands, they become conductors of heavenly energies, you can use them to introduce energy into the water you are about to drink. Fill a glass with pure water (mountain spring water if possible), hold it in your left hand and dip the three fingers of your right hand (thumb, index and major) in it whilst concentrating on love, wisdom and truth: you will impregnate the water with those things. Then drink it, thinking, 'This is love that heals, this is wisdom that enlightens, this is truth that liberates.'

Initiates use water to cure illness. They write on a piece of paper certain Kabalistic terms that link them with the higher entities, then they magnetize the paper and bum it. The person who is ill is given water to drink containing the ashes and... is cured.

Water has always played a big part in religion, the Jews immersed themselves in the Jordan River, the Hindus in the Ganges, and baptism by water is an important part of the Christian religion. Nowadays men have forgotten the meaning behind those practices, they no longer know how to communicate with the higher forces, but you, dear brothers and sisters, can now learn to open the pores of your soul and absorb the spiritual elements the water contains.

Sèvres, 30th January, 1945

Notes
1. See *The Mysteries of Fire and Water,* Izvor Coll. n° 232, chap. 1: 'The Two Principles of Creation, Water and Fire'.
2. See *Sons and Daughters of God,* Izvor Coll. n° 240, chap. 12: 'Out of his belly shall flow Rivers of living water'.

Question: 'Master, would you tell us what purifying exercises can be done while bathing?'

Most people do not know that they can purify their etheric and astral bodies with water. Etheric and astral impurities are very difficult to get rid of, those of the astral plane are the most powerful and harmful of all. Water chases away these impurities, if it has first been vivified. To do that, you take a quantity of salt (you know the important part salt plays in religious rites) that you have consecrated (by lighting candles, burning incense and pronouncing formulas) to purity, to the Divine Mother, to Cosmic Spirit, and you ask the celestial Intelligences to bless the salt and confer healing virtues on it.

Salt is often mentioned in the sacred books but its importance has never really been understood. It says in the *Gospels, 'Ye are the salt of the earth, but if the salt hath lost his savour, wherewith shall it be salted? It is thenceforth good for nothing but to be cast out and to be trodden under foot of men.'* [1] To the alchemists, salt, sulphur and mercury were essential to their operations. Of course, the salt I am speaking of is not kitchen salt but the product of the union of the two principles, the masculine (acid) and the feminine (the base) which produce the child (salt). Salt has a profound significance for those who know how to use it.

Therefore, before getting into the bath, throw in the salt you have prepared and pronounce a few words to sanctify the water by virtue of the salt. Then say to the Divine Mother, 'O Divine Mother, how I admire this water that reflects Thee! I pray Thee, sanctify it so that all impurity may be washed away and I may serve my Heavenly Father.' Dip your hand in the water and talk to the creatures that live in it, 'O ondines, how beautiful you are, how transparent and pure! Take away everything in me that is harmful or that is not in harmony with Heaven!' Then touch the water with love.

Water contains living entities as beautiful and pure as they are invisible that put you in contact with extremely sensitive Beings, who become favourably disposed toward you because of your loving attitude. As you step into the water tell it how beautiful it is, how much it delights and amazes you, soap yourself three times and pour the water you have previously set aside in a pitcher over yourself: if you have love and faith, you will obtain great results, it all depends on how much faith and love you have.

Formulas for consecrating salt and water are known to have existed in all the ancient tongues, proving that this practice goes back a long way. Why the formulas? Emanations are the universal language that all spirits know how to translate, the colours man emanates are the expression of his thoughts and feelings, a language that the invisible creatures grasp immediately, with no need for words.[2] But the physical plane is different, words are very important here, and that is the reason for formulas. If you think a formula without pronouncing it aloud, the forces will accumulate on the mental plane, but there will be no realization on the physical plane.

Words are a signature: a paper has no value unless it is signed, an army launches an attack only when the signal is given by the general, and you must pronounce words to release forces in the physical sphere: before the invisible forces can go into action words are necessary. This has never been properly understood by spiritualists: it is something the disciple must know about and act on.

No one really knows what purity is. People take a bath every day but never think of removing the inner impurities. Our desire and greed form fluidic layers that interfere with the smooth flow of heavenly currents and emanations and these impurities must be removed. Water can do it if you connect with the subtle forces of the Universe in thought and use the proper words. You will not succeed immediately but if you keep trying, in time you will be free, for water absorbs bad things as well as good ones. That is why when you are in the midst of joy and wonderment, you should not wash or bathe, but if you take a bath when you are unhappy, you will feel better because the water absorbs your sadness.

Of course it isn't possible to perform the exercise I have described in a wash basin, but you could say, 'As I wash my physical face, may my spiritual face be washed,' and then pray for a minute.

Amongst the many things you will learn from the esoteric Science is that the physical body has greater power when naked: words pronounced then are more powerful. For what reason? I am not permitted to tell you, the risk is too great, but witches for instance, execute their magic rites naked because their power is then at its most intense.

The world is caught in such a mesh of materialism that there is no time for purity. All our physical and psychic troubles stem from not getting rid of impure elements. In order to help humans, the Initiates sometimes take upon themselves their impurities and transform them.

When you fall ill or are indisposed, you should consider it a sign, the invisible world is inviting you to work on purifying yourself. Accept this inconvenience with gratitude, knowing that you would not have thought of it otherwise. When little impurities manifest themselves, do something immediately to remedy them or at least take precautions. Once impurities accumulate (without your knowing it because there is no manifestation), it will be almost impossible for you to get rid of them.

Some people are made ill by the slightest impurity in their food or in the air, showing that they are very pure; others who eat meat, drink alcohol and smoke a great deal have a system so saturated with impurities that they are completely insensitive to bad smells, smoke and noise. Those who live in the midst of purity immediately sense these discomforts.

This is the advice I ask you to follow: consider all minor physical disturbances such as itching, pimples, stomach and headaches, etc., as a sign that you should work on purifying yourself. Consider these things as an opportunity to work, to exert yourself and get rid of some impurity that will drag a lot of others along with it. Purification! No one works on purity and that is why things get worse and worse for mankind. The Initiates do not ask to be left in peace. Heaven sends them all kinds of inconveniences and drawbacks to oblige them to keep advancing by purifying themselves.

Sèvres, 3rd July, 1970

Notes
1. See *The Philosopher's Stone – in the Gospels and in Alchemy,* Izvor Coll. n° 241, chap. 3: 'You are the salt of the earth' and chap. 4: 'But if the salt loses its flavour'.
2. See *Notre peau spirituelle, l'aura,* Brochure n° 309, and *The Path of Silence,* Izvor Coll. n° 229, chap. 10: 'Speech and the Logos'.

Chapter Four

THE TRUE BAPTISM

Every day you must think about purifying yourself. Don't tell me you did it yesterday or the day before... yesterday's work was for yesterday, today you must begin again. You must have in mind this cleansing and purification, this sanctification, every day, the work must be done daily until your whole being becomes renewed.

People imagine that because they were baptized they are pure and holy for the rest of their lives. It is a good thing to be baptized, but if you think the evil spirits will leave you alone because your forehead has been anointed with a little holy water or oil, you are mistaken. The devils enter where they like without fear, they are not impressed with the baptismal ceremony. It is man himself who must do the work of conserving and amplifying the effects of his baptism; if he does not, there will not be much effect. Try and explain that to Christians! Christians are hardheaded, they believe in the absolute efficacity of baptism as they believe they are saved once and for all because Jesus shed his blood for them: they can sin all they like, they have been saved once and for all! I ask, 'In that case why are men ill and unhappy? Why are they still paying off debts if Jesus has paid for them?'[1] There is no answer.

When you are baptized your sins are washed away, but only if you work all your life to foster what was deposited in you at your baptism. You must cleanse yourself each day, consciously, with all your heart and soul. Some people are so proud and satisfied at being baptized they think they don't need to do anything more, but when you see the way they live, you realize that they are exactly like those who have not been baptized. To them I say, 'You haven't understood, you haven't learned, your baptism and Jesus have not saved you... you must do something to save yourself'

When you read the Old Testament, you see that the Prophet Elisha told Naaman that if he plunged into the Jordan River seven times, he would be healed of leprosy. And Jesus also was baptized in the Jordan, by John the Baptist. The ablutions of baptism are effective depending to a great extent on the spiritual level of the person officiating. The same is true for talismans,[2] the power of a talisman depends on the person who prepares it. If he is ignorant, the talisman will have no effect because it received no force, an object becomes a talisman only when impregnated with the Telesma force. Telesma, 'the most forceful force of all forces' as Hermes Trismegistus calls it in his Emerald Tablet, fills the talisman with power. Without it, the object is there but Telesma is not, and it is not a real talisman.

Water is a magic element where purification is concerned because beings who live and work through the water are able to remove fluidic layers that are impure. It is good to immerse oneself in water, but the most important thing is to be conscious of its power. If the water has been blessed and magnetized, or if an Initiate has consecrated it by pronouncing certain formulas, then yes, it will be effective. But even then its power does not last forever, a person may be delivered for a while from his troubles or obsessions, but later he will fall back into the same negative states because the purification came from outside. Purification is lasting only if the person involved does not keep making the same mistakes. He must keep himself pure in thought, pure in feeling and pure in action; his purification will be lasting only on that condition.

In the spiritual life, no external means ever has a lasting effect if the man himself does not live a pure and meaningful life. Humans have illusions on this subject because nobody explains the truth to them. The cross is supposed to be beneficial for instance, and so everyone wears a cross. Yes, but has a cross the power to save one from sickness, or from his own weaknesses? I know people who wear crosses who are nevertheless in a dreadful state... why does the cross not save them? Because a cross should be worn inwardly in the form of a quality, a virtue;[3] only then will it be effective, beneficial, magic. A cross made of gold or ivory or anything else and worn externally can do nothing to help you. If you magnetize the cross by putting your faith and love into it, and you are linked to the Christ, then yes, it has extraordinary power.

Christians wear crosses, light candles,[4] use rosaries, but do nothing to put life into these objects, which makes it all slightly ridiculous. People must stop believing in dead things, and realize that it is up to them to put life into these things.

One day people will see that there is no cause to be proud of having been baptized a Catholic, for it is not enough. We must become and remain catholic all our lives, but not the way a child is baptized a Catholic without having an opinion on the subject, when he grows up he may prefer to be a Taoist or whatever. Don't be shocked, I say these things to you in order to give you a larger comprehension. You can be a baptized Catholic, Protestant, or Orthodox, but if you live a life that is somewhere between an animal life and a human life, what good is baptism?

No, dear brothers and sisters, do not content yourself with having been baptized a Catholic. Say to yourself, 'I must become really catholic, that is, universal, with no division, hatred, or hostility in my heart but with the conviction that all men are God's children.' For the moment you still think that those who belong to another religion than yours are not God's children and should be rejected. That is where you are not catholic... If you were, in spite of your difference of opinion you would embrace all men with the conviction that they are all sons of God.

The Bonfin, 22nd September, 1972

Notes
1. See *Sons and Daughters of God,* Izvor Coll. n° 240, chap. 11: 'Jesus' sacrifice on the cross: the powers of blood'.
2. See *The Book of Divine Magic,* Izvor Coll. n° 226, chap. 5: 'Talismans'.
3. See *The Symbolic Language of Geometrical Figures,* Izvor Coll. n° 218, chap. 6: 'The Cross'.
4. See *The Mysteries of Fire and Water,* Izvor Coll. n° 232, chap. 13: 'A Candle Flame'.

Chapter Five

THE ANGELS OF THE FOUR ELEMENTS

Today I will talk to you about how to correlate the breathing exercises we do each morning with the Angels of the four elements. I have not given you this exercise before because it requires preparation to do it correctly, and most of you are not ready.

You know about the four Angels and the elements they govern which are actually sixteen rather than four, because earth, water, air and fire exist also in the physical, astral, mental, and spiritual or causal worlds. We will come to the causal world a little later.

Kether, the highest realm, is where the four Holy Beasts are, the *Seraphim*[1] who govern the four elements... not the fire, air, water, and earth elements as we know them which are no more than pale reflections or condensations of the higher substance in the heart of the Everlasting God... but the substance, the garment of the Lord that allows Him to manifest, the inconceivably tenuous pure matter referred to by alchemists as the primeval Waters.

In the Kabala it says that the Absolute God is inconceivable, imperceptible, incognizable for us except insofar as He manifests Himself. God emanates His own substance, which is why the Kabalists say there are two aspects of God, manifest and non-manifest.

I have studied the cosmogonies of the world's religions and I find them dispersed, disparate, not one gives the idea of the Creation as clearly and lucidly as the Kabala. The Kabalistic system as far as I am concerned is the best, the most concise and the only mathematically precise system.

The Kabalists explain the Creation with a system of ten Sephiroth leading up to the unknown region beyond *Kether* called *Ain Soph Aur* or infinite light (*Ain* = without, *Soph* = End, *Aur* = light: light without end)[2] which is the inconceivable, unattainable, indescribable abyss. Some humans have gone all the way to these regions but the ideas they came back with belong to an order beyond our comprehension... if we cannot imagine *Kether*, how can we imagine something even higher: *Ain Soph Aur.*

Hence, in the Kabalistic tradition, God the Absolute clothes Himself in a pure, most subtle substance in order to manifest Himself. That substance is symbolized by the four Holy Beasts in *Kether*, the Principles of matter, the four Elements that have nothing to do with the four elements of our Universe for they are beyond human conception.

According to the Kabala, when God was impelled to create the Universe He first formed His Kingdom, *Atziluth,* comprising the Atmic, Buddhic, and Causal worlds. *Atziluth* is the glorious divine world, the world of pure Idea where the Seraphim, Cherubim and Thrones live in the Sephiroth *Kether* (the Crown), *Chokmah* (Wisdom), and *Binah* (Intelligence). The emanations of *Atziluth* formed the region called *Beriah* (the Creation) or world of the Intellect, comprising the Sephiroth *Chesed* (Mercy), *Geburah* (Severity), and *Tiphareth* (Beauty). *Atziluth* is the first world of spirit and soul; the second world, *Beriah,* the world of the Intellect, emanated the dense matter that formed *Ietzirah* (Formation), the third or astral world comprising the Sephiroth *Netzach* (Victory), *Hod* (Glory), and *Yesod* (the Foundation). The first world is the divine world, the second is the mental, spiritual world, the third is the much denser astral world, and the fourth is *Asiah,* the physical world with the Sephira *Malkuth* (the Kingdom).[3]

The Creation is divided by the Kabalists into the number 4. Other esoterists divide it into 3 or 7 or 10 or 12... each one has its own particular significance without contradicting the others. The alchemists also use 4, the Hindus and Theosophists use 7, the astrologers use 12, the Christians and Egyptians use 3 (the Trinity), the Persians use 2 (dualism) while still others use 1 (monism). It would take too long to explain the reason for these divisions, I already have in other lectures; today I want to talk about the 4 of the Kabalists and alchemists.

The Kabalists divide the Universe into 4 regions: the physical world *Asiah,* the astral world *Iezirah,* the mental world *Beriah,* and finally the world of emanations and the spirit, *Atziluth.* *Atziluth* contains the Angels of the four Principles of matter, the four-faced *Cherubim,* one with the face of a bull, one with the face of a man, one with the face of an eagle and one with that of a lion, as seen by St. John, the Prophet Ezekiel, and others... as well as the four Angels of the mental world, the four Angels of the astral world, and the four Angels of the physical world. When we address the Angel of Air, the Angel of Water, the Angel of Fire or the Angel of the Earth, we are addressing the four Angels of the region *Asiah* who govern the water, wind, fire and earth that we know and perceive. Is that clear? The four Angels of the physical world and the four elements we perceive in our Universe must not be confused with the four Holy Beasts who are the Principles of matter. The fire we know is not the real fire above, there are several kinds of fire and the fire we light and that burns here is not the same as the fire of the sun.[4]

The sublime Angels are too far beyond us to be attainable, we cannot even attract their attention. Some people have the pretention of searching for the Absolute; they should not try, the Absolute cannot be found. A disciple should begin by trying to reach great beings like the Saints, the Prophets, the Initiates and great Masters who have an interest in humans. Later he may go higher and invoke the angels, who are the nearest to humans in the angelic Hierarchy and can hear us and help us if they wish. The disciple might even go on to invoke the Archangels, but there is no use trying to be heard by the Principalities or the hosts of higher Angels. The angelic Hierarchies have work to do in the innumerable worlds of infinite space and the billions of creatures living there, and have nothing to do with humans. The ones that do take care of humans are the Saints and Patriarchs, the Initiates, the Masters, the Apostles, the Prophets, that is, those who have lived on earth and remember the promises they may have made, the relations they had. A disciple should realize that the angelic Hierarchies exist but if he wants results he must address his prayers and meditations to beings who are nearer to him.

The great Initiates go higher and explore the sublime regions, they even speak with the *Hachmalim, Aralim, Ophanim,* and higher still, the *Hayoth haKadesh,* in order to work for the future of humanity. But the disciple should not attempt to go so high... he will simply fall asleep. I tell you these things so that you will not imagine that you will have immediate access to the *Seraphim, the Cherubim,* or the *Thrones.* No, this is a very long and arduous path for which you are not ready, but you can reach the Angels. The Angels still take care of matter for their realm is *Yesod,* and *Yesod* is the nearest Sephira to *Malkuth,* the earth.

The divine world, *Atziluth,* comprises the Sephiroth *Kether, Chokmah,* and *Binah.* The world of Intelligence, *Beriah,* comprises the Sephiroth *Chesed, Geburah,* and *Tiphareth.* The Sephiroth *Netzach, Hod* and *Yesod* represent the astral world, *Ietzirah,* and *Malkuth* represents *Asiah,* the physical world. 'Why is there but one Sephira for the physical sphere?' you ask. Because it is a very big Sephira, a condensation of all the others. *Malkuth* is the summary, the reflection and concretization of all the other Sephiroth and is divided in 4 divisions that

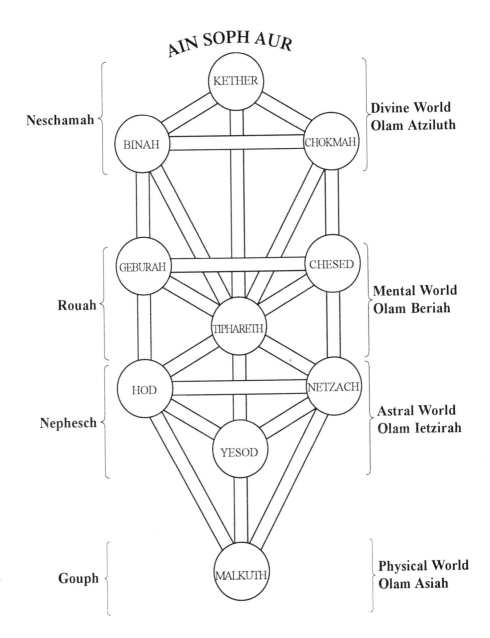

TREE OF LIFE

correspond with the four elements. That is why it appears on the Sephirotic Tree, the Tree of Life with four colours (red, green, blue, yellow) whereas the others only have one. The four colours represent the four states of matter: solid (red), liquid (green), gaseous (blue) and igneous (yellow).

The Kabala also shows us how these four regions are reflected in man. The physical body is called *gouph* and the astral body, *nephesch*. The word *nephesch* resembles the word *nahash* (serpent) and chanah, the cycle of the year, but I will talk to you some other time on that subject. Then comes *rouah* meaning spirit, but spirit on the mental plane, and lastly *neschamah,* which corresponds to the world of the soul and spirit. The regions that are still higher and still more subtle than *neschamah* are called *Hayah* and *Iehidah* by the Kabala, and the causal, Buddhic and Atmic bodies in the Hindu religion. The Kabalists divide man into four parts: *gouph, nephesch, rouah,* and neschamah, the same as the universe. Without going into details, which is not possible at the moment, this will give you a precise idea of the way the Kabala divides the different regions.

The breathing exercises we do each morning also are based on the number 4: 4-16-8 and 8-32-16. We began the exercises to the rhythm: 4-16-8, and later went on to 8-32-16, which means that you breathe in to the count of 8, hold your breath to the count of 32, and exhale to the count of 16. Maybe later on we will do the exercise to the count of 16-64-32, but first you must learn to breathe better, that is, not with the upper part of the lungs as you do now, but down in the stomach. If you do this exercise every day, your lungs will expand and become stronger.

When I was in India I was amazed at the huge stomachs of the sadhus and yogis. There are two reasons for this, it can be that one is lazy and sedentary and eats too much, or it can be because of breathing exercises repeated regularly... which is the case of the yogis: from breathing deeply, they develop the diaphragm and stomach. Statues of the Buddha all show him with a prominent stomach.

The purity of the system depends on respiration. The blood courses through the body to the lungs where it is purified and if you do the breathing exercises consciously every day, you will little by little purify your entire system. During the exercises you should work with your mind to attract the substance, forces and particles of the higher world, that is, light and peace and other vital elements you lack and wish to attract.

For instance, you might choose four virtues and repeat the word for each one 16 times (4 for each one) as you hold your breath and concentrate on climbing up through the Sephiroth, or through your own physical, astral, mental, and causal bodies, whichever suits you best.

And then you exhale... which is what I want to talk to you about today... while calling on the Angels of the 4 elements. Your imagination is hard at work forming images while you exhale to the count of 16: for the 4 first counts you imagine that the fire is passing through your head removing all the dark shadows, and thus the Angel of Fire sanctifies you; for 4 more counts you imagine that your lungs are filled with a spiritual breath of air sent by the Angel of Air to purify you; during the next 4 counts you imagine a crystal clear water pouring through your stomach, intestins, liver, spleen, sexual organs... the Angel of Water washes you clean. And finally you imagine all the waste matter in your entire body being absorbed into the earth as the Angel of Earth cleanses your body. This exercise takes very little time once you get in the habit. Fire purifies the brain, Air purifies the lungs, Water purifies the stomach and sex, and the Earth purifies the whole body by taking away everything that keeps it from functioning properly. A tremendously effective exercise!

What have you done for Heaven, dear brothers and sisters, to deserve the privilege of hearing and learning these things?

Of course until you try them out, you cannot realize their value. These are the very same methods the Initiates use to purify and sanctify themselves. Even if humans are not capable of perceiving purity, other creatures in the astral or mental plane do notice: when a being who is really pure passes by, he projects sparks of light into space.

The exercise I have just described is one of the best but I warn you not to overtax your brain... it is still fragile and must be treated with care. Some of the brothers and sisters throw themselves wholeheartedly into the exercises, overdo them and fall ill. If you try to force things, your brain will refuse, nothing will work. Your thoughts are vagabonds by nature, they love to roam; for that reason you should leave them alone at first and then very gently start your brain working, exactly as you let the motor warm up before driving your car. Start by thinking about something good and positive, no matter what, and then lead your thoughts into the direction you want them to take. They will obey you if you begin this way but if you try to dominate them too suddenly and without ceremony, they will rebel and go off on their own! That is why many brothers and sisters have no results in their attempts at meditation.

You must be very intelligent, very diplomatic with your thoughts and this is hard to do, but once you know how to control them you will be able to do a tremendously powerful work all day long in the same vein. It will take one day to do the work that ordinarily took several, and you will never tire. People who try to force things impede the proper functioning of their brain and end up with nothing but headache... and then they give up trying to meditate. Do you remember, I took my time explaining things to you before we started these exercises, and those who understood and trusted me then, can now do the work and obtain results. It is not my fault if some of you forgot my instructions and cannot do the exercises, I have given my brothers and sisters all the explanations they need.

Be careful not to overcharge your nervous system, tension is bad for the nervous system. If you can master the exercise I have just given you, it will open up great possibilities for you. Think slowly and deliberately about the purest fire, the purest air, the purest water, and the earth opening up and absorbing all your impurities.

We are surrounded by magic agents, all around us there is water, air, earth, fire... God has put extraordinary powers in these elements for our use: we should avail ourselves of them.

Thank Heaven for letting you listen to these truths in this limpid atmosphere, this peace, this purity, this silence. In the sun.

May light and peace be with you!

The Bonfin, 14th July, 1969

Notes
1. See *Angels and other Mysteries of the Tree of Life,* Izvor Coll. n° 236, chap. 2: 'Introduction to the Sephirotic Tree of Life' and chap. 3: 'The Angelic Hierarchies'.
2. Op. cit., chap. 6: 'Ain Soph Aur, Unlimited Light'.
3. Op. cit., chap. 7: 'Light, the Substance of the Universe' and chap. 8: 'When God Drew a Circle on the Face of the Deep'.
4. See *The Splendour of Tiphareth,* Complete Works, vol. 10, chap. 21: 'Three Kinds of Fire'.

BIBLICAL REFERENCES

Part I
'Take it and eat it up, it shall make thy belly bitter' – *Revel. 10 : 9, p. 21.*
'I am Alpha and Omega' – *Revel. 1 : 8 and 22 : 13, p. 21.*

Part II, Chapter 2
'Go and sin no more !' – *John 8 : 11, p. 38.*

Part II, Chapter 4
'Holy, Holy, Holy, Lord God Almighty' – *Revel. 4 : 8, p. 58.*
'Lord, create in me a pure and contrite heart' – *Ps. 51 : 12-13, p. 58.*
'Our Father which art in Heaven' – *Matt. 6 : 10, p. 58.*
'Eternal (The) Life is to know Thee...' – *John 17 : 3, p. 59.*
'Thy Will be done on earth as it is in Heaven' – *Matt. 6 : 10, p. 60.*
'Whatsoever ye would that men should do to you, do ye even so to them' – *Luke 6 : 31, p. 65.*
Adulteress (The) – *John 8 : 1-11, p. 65.*
'I am come that they might have abundant life' – *John 10 : 10, p. 67.*
Jesus tells his disciples that he will send them the Spirit
　John 16 : 13, p. 67.
'There is nothing from without a man that entering into him'
　Matt. 15 : 11, p. 71.
'Ye are the Temple of the Living God' – *Paul II Cor. 6 : 16, p. 68.*

Part II, Chapter 5
Archangel (The) Gabriel appears before Mary to announce the birth of Jesus – *Luke 1 : 11-20, p. 73.*
Archangel (The) Gabriel appears before Zachariah to annonce the birth of John the Baptist – *Luke 1 : 11-20, p. 73.*
'I am the way, the truth and the life' – *John 10 : 10, p. 74.*
Dragon (The) bound for a thousand years – *Revel. 20 : 1-4, p. 78.*

Part II, Chapter 6
'He is my refuge and my fortress' – *Ps. 91, p. 88.*

World Wide - Editor-Distributor
Editions Prosveta S.A. - Z.A. Le Capitou - B.P. 12
F - 83601 Fréjus CEDEX (France)
Tel. (33) 04 94 19 33 33 – Fax (33) 04 94 19 33 34
Web: www.prosveta.com – e-mail: international@prosveta.com

Distributors

ARGENTINA
ASOCIACIÓN SOPHIA – Chile 1736 – Ciudad Mendoza
Tel (54) 261 420 10 47 – e-mail: info@sophia.org.ar

AUSTRALIA
PROSVETA AUSTRALIA
6/A Tyneside Avenue – North Willoughby – Sydney NSW 2068
Tel. (61) (0) 2 8197 1006
e-mail: prosveta.au@bigpond.com

AUSTRIA
HARMONIEQUELL VERSAND – Hof 37 – A- 5302 Henndorf am Wallersee
Tel. / fax (43) 6214 7413 – e-mail: info@prosveta.at

BELGIUM & LUXEMBOURG
PROSVETA BENELUX – Beeldenmakersstraat 1 – B 8000 Brugge
Tel./Fax. (32)(0)50/61 69 10 – e-mail: prosveta@skynet.be
N.V. MAKLU Somersstraat 13-15 – B-2000 Antwerpen
Tel. (32) 3/231 29 00 – Fax (32) 3/233 26 59
S.D.L. CARAVELLE S.A. – rue du Pré aux Oies, 303 – 1130 Bruxelles
Tel. (32) 2 240 93 00 – Fax (32) 2 216 35 98
e-mail : info@sdlcaravelle.com

BOLIVIA
BELTRÁN – Calle Muñoz Cornejo, Sopocachi – La Paz
e-mail: mariabelre@yahoo.es

BULGARIA
SVETOGLED – Bd Saborny 16 A, appt 11 – 9000 Varna
e-mail: vassil100@abv.bg – Tel/Fax: (359) 52 63 90 94

CANADA
PROSVETA Inc. – 3950, Albert Mines – Canton-de-Hatley (Qc), J0B 2C0
Tel. (819) 564-8212 – Fax. (819) 564-1823 – *in Canada,* call toll free: 1-800-854-8212
e-mail: prosveta@prosveta-canada.com / www.prosveta-canada.com

COLOMBIA
AFBU COLOMBIA
Calle 146 N° 13-10, Apto 404 Interior 2 – Bogotá, Colombia
Tel. (57)16 14 53 85 – Fax. (57)16 33 58 03 – Celular: (57) 311 810 25 42
e-mail: kalagiya@hotmail.com

CONGO
PROSVETA CONGO
29, Avenue de la Révolution – B.P. 768 – Pointe-Noire
Tel. : (242) 948156 / (242) 5531254 – Fax : (242) 948156
e-mail: prosvetacongo@yahoo.fr

CYPRUS
THE SOLAR CIVILISATION BOOKSHOP – BOOKBINDING
73 D Kallipoleos Avenue – Lycavitos – P. O. Box 24947, 1355 – Nicosia
e-mail: cypapach@cytanet.com.cy – Tel / Fax 00357-22-377503

CZECH REPUBLIC
PROSVETA – Ant. Sovy 18 – České Budejovice 370 05
Tel / Fax: (420) 38-53 10 227 – e-mail: prosveta@iol.cz

FRANCE – DOM TOM
Editions Prosveta S.A. - B.P. 12 – F - 83601 Fréjus CEDEX (France)
Tel. (33) 04 94 19 33 33 – Fax (33) 04 94 19 33 34
e-mail: international@prosveta.com – www.prosveta.com

GERMANY
PROSVETA Verlag GmbH – Heerstrasse 55 – 78628 Rottweil
Tel. (49) 741-46551 – Fax. (49) 741-46552 – e-mail: prosveta7@aol.com

GREAT BRITAIN – IRELAND
PROSVETA – The Doves Nest, Duddleswell Uckfield – East Sussex TN 22 3JJ
Tel. (44) (01825) 712988 – Fax (44) (01825) 713386 – e-mail: prosveta@pavilion.co.uk

HAITI
PROSVETA DÉPÔT HAITI – Angle rue Faustin 1er et rue Bois Patate #25 bis
6110 Port-au-Prince
Tel. (509) 245 06 43 – Mobile: (509) 464 80 88 – e-mail: rbaaudant@yahoo.com

HOLLAND
STICHTING PROSVETA NEDERLAND
Zeestraat 50 – 2042 LC Zandvoort
Tel. (31) 33 25 345 75 – Fax. (31) 33 25 803 20 – e-mail: prosveta@worldonline.nl

ISRAEL
Zohar, P.B. 1046, Netanya 42110 – e-mail: prosveta.il@hotmail.com

ITALY
PROSVETA Coop. a r.l.
Casella Postale 55 – 06068 Tavernelle (PG)
Tel. (39) 075-835 84 98 – Fax (39) 075-835 97 12 – e-mail: prosveta@tin.it

IVORY COAST
Librairie Prosveta
25 rue Paul Langevin Zone 4C – 01 Abidjan
e-mail: prosvetafrique@yahoo.fr – Tel/Fax: (225) 21 25 42 11

LEBANON
PROSVETA LIBAN – P.O. Box 90-995
Jdeidet-el-Metn, Beirut – Tel. (03) 448560 – e-mail: prosveta_lb@terra.net.lb

NORWAY
PROSVETA NORDEN – Postboks 318, N-1502 Moss
Tel. (47) 69 26 51 40 – Fax (47) 69 26 51 08 – e-mail: info@prosveta.no

PORTUGAL
EDIÇÕES PROSVETA
Rua Palmira 66 r/c - C – 1170 - 287 Lisboa
Tel. / Fax (351) 213 540 764 – e-mail: prosvetapt@hotmail.com

ROMANIA
ANTAR – Str. N. Constantinescu 10 – Bloc 16A - sc A - Apt. 9
Sector 1 – 71253 Bucarest
Tel. 004021-231 28 78 – Tel./ Fax 004021-231 37 19
e-mail : prosveta_ro@yahoo.com

RUSSIA
EDITIONS PROSVETA
143 964 Moskovskaya oblast, g. Reutov – 4, post/box 4
Tel./ Fax. (095) 525 18 17 – Tel. (095) 795 70 74 – e-mail: prosveta@online.ru

SERBIE
ÉDITIONS GLOSARIJUM *(for the Serbia Language)*
Rige od Fere 12 – Beograd
Tél./Fax 011/2182-163 – e-mail: glosarijum@glosarijum.com

SPAIN
ASOCIACIÓN PROSVETA ESPAÑOLA – C/ Ausias March n° 23 Ático
SP-08010 Barcelona – Tel (34) (93) 412 31 85 – Fax (34) (93) 318 89 01
e-mail: aprosveta@prosveta.es

UNITED STATES
PROSVETA US Dist.
26450 Ruether Ave #205 – Santa Clarita CA 91350
Tel. (661) 251-5412 – Fax. (661) 252-1751
e-mail: prosveta-usa@earthlink.net. / www.prosveta-usa.com
SWITZERLAND
PROSVETA Société Coopérative
Ch. de la Céramone 2 – CH - 1808 Les Monts-de-Corsier
Tel. (41) 21 921 92 18 – Fax. (41) 21 922 92 04
e-mail: prosveta@bluewin.ch
VENEZUELA
PROSVETA VENEZUELA C. A. – Calle Madrid
Edificio La Trinidad – Las Mercedes – Caracas D.F.
Tel. (58) 414 134 75 34 – e-mail: prosvetavenezuela@gmail.com

*Updated list 11.12.07. If you cannot contact one of these distributors,
consult the internet site www.prosveta.com*

The aim of the Universal White Brotherhood association
is the study and practice of the Teaching
of Master Omraam Mikhaël Aïvanhov,
published and distributed
by Prosveta.
All enquiries about the association should be addressed to:
Universal White Brotherhood
The Doves Nest, Duddleswell, Uckfield
East Sussex TN22 3JJ, GREAT BRITAIN
Tel: (44) (0)1825 712150 – Fax: (44) (0)1825 713386
E-mail: uwb@pavilion.co.uk

Printed in March 2008
by PULSIO Ltd
19 Tvardishki Prohod – 1404 Sofia – Bulgaria

Dépôt légal: Mars 2008
1er dépôt légal dans la même collection: 1978